The Children of the Nation

An Anthology of Working People's Poetry from Contemporary Ireland

Edited and introduced by
Jenny Farrell

Foreword by Brian Campfield

De dheasca an ú
Is iomaí créatúr gan
Ach a bhfuil uime ina
Tá mílte ina mogha a
Is an síol calctha I mbl

Because of usu
Many creatures have n
Except for the clothes on their backs,
Need has slaves by the thousand,
The seed has clogged in the loins of the land.

— Máirtín Ó Direáin (1910-1988)

First published in 2019 by **Culture Matters Co-Operative Ltd.**
Culture Matters promotes a socialist and progressive approach to art, culture and politics. See www.culturematters.org.uk

Acknowledgements
Culture Matters is grateful for the support and assistance of Fórsa, UNITE, CWU, Mandate, and the Belfast and Galway Trades Councils.

Foreword

By *Brian Campfield*
General Secretary of the Northern Ireland Public Services Alliance,
2010-2015 and President of the Irish Congress
of Trade Unions, 2015-2017

In the trade union movement, we understandably concentrate our efforts on collective actions to advance the interests of working people, both in the workplace and in our interventions in the public and political arenas. Underlying our collective actions is an understanding that we are also involved in a movement which challenges the hollowing-out of democracy, and it is no surprise that in addition to the struggle for a fairer share of the fruits of labour, we find ourselves in conflict with those interests which promote an even greater extension of private sector interests through privatisation and the commercialisation of public services. We are well aware that the struggles of working people and their hopes and aspirations are constantly marginalised.

We also understand that the creative articulation of working-class experiences contributes to a more developed awareness and self-confidence among working people, and therefore I was delighted to be asked to become involved in assisting **Culture Matters** publish this anthology of working-class poetry in Ireland. The support of a number of Irish trade union organisations, North and South, has provided a rare opportunity to publish the work of poets who regard their work as expressions of working-class experiences and conditions.

The response in terms of the number and quality of submissions, and the variety of themes and styles represented, can only be described as phenomenal. At the same time, I am convinced that this response only scratches the surface and that there are many more poets, whose works shed important light and insights into the lives of ordinary people, who may not have been aware of the call for submissions. So although this is the first anthology if its kind to be published, I hope that it is not the last.

The anthology is inclusive and egalitarian, and values authenticity, relevance and communicativeness as well as literary skill and inventiveness. A platform has been created which enables artistic expressions of a range of themes experienced from working-class perspectives to be not only articulated, but brought to life in print. The anthology is grounded in individual effort, but has transformed these individual endeavours into a collective expression of the lives, aspirations, concerns and hopes of that class in our society which

i

constantly has to struggle to get its voice heard and valued, and its interests represented, in mainstream publishing and public discourse generally.

It is also heartening that the anthology includes poems in both the Irish and English languages. Perhaps a further edition might attract poems in other languages which reflect the experiences of the many ethnic minorities who have in more recent years found themselves working and living in Ireland.

For all these reasons, I sincerely welcome this pioneering anthology as a good example of the application of the principles of cultural democracy to poetry publishing. I feel sure that readers will not only enjoy the poems but also gain valuable, sympathetic insights into the lives, struggles and preoccupations of working people in this country through the medium of poetry. Readers may also be encouraged and inspired to write something themselves, hopefully!

Belfast, August 2019

Introduction

By Jenny Farrell, Department of Languages & Humanities, Galway-Mayo Institute of Technology and Associate Editor, Culture Matters

Just as societies today are rooted in classes, those who exploit and those who are exploited, so too there exist two cultures, divided along the same lines. There is the dominant, mainstream culture, which reinforces the views of the ruling class, and then there is a plebeian, democratic, socialist culture—the expression of the experiences of the working class, of the dispossessed.

As humans, we grapple with the world around us in artistic ways—and we have done so since we produced cave paintings. Other artistic expressions from all those millennia ago have not survived, nor could have, like music, song and dance, storytelling. Naturally, this did not cease after tribal societies developed into class societies. In contrast to written history, art achieves the sensuous access to human life. It puts us in touch with the individual person, their thoughts, feelings, experiences from long ago, or our own days.

Class societies evolved when improved production techniques created more than was needed for immediate survival of the tribe, a surplus product. This allowed over time a small group to take over the means of production, become idle, and to exploit and rule over the many who produced their community's wealth. From then on, the ideas of those who owned the wealth, those who ruled, determined how their society was represented in the arts. Many, but not all artists obliged. However, there were also the artists of the people who were not part of the establishment culture. This art communicates their struggle for liberation, and their hopes for a humane society of equals, a society that is fit for humankind. This art survives in the oral tradition, folktales or for example the Gospels of the slaves. With the evolution of the working class both rural and industrial, it too records its experiences and struggles.

To use an example from Ireland, when collecting poems by the working people on their experience of the 1798 rebellion, it was noted: *"The loss of so many Gaelic texts has resulted in a lack of insight into the views of the rebel rank and file."* In Ulster, the weaver poets of the late 18th century worked in the textiles industry. They wrote in their native dialect, and in this way broke with the aesthetic norms of their day. Some of them were involved in the 1798 rising.

The establishment mocked and suppressed the working-class voices. They were not published and it is surprising and often down to coincidence, or the insight and courage of individuals, that these documents did not end up on the rubbish pile of history. The story of the first working-class novel, Robert Tressell's *The Ragged-Trousered Philanthropists*, is just one example, and many mainstream publishers still consider the working-class voice unwanted and unsellable.

An anthology of this kind is needed, a collection of poetry specifically focused on the experience of the working class, the unemployed, the precariously employed, the homeless, and other groups who are excluded from the mainstream. Writing in Irish is another field where publishers are reluctant to print the darker stories. While individual working-class writers have published collections of their own work, we believe this anthology of sixty-seven poets to be unique in its exclusive focus on working people's poetry from contemporary Ireland.

Our understanding of 'working class' is as follows. In antagonistic class society, the working class is comprised of those people who possess nothing but their labour power. They are in an exploitative relationship with the owners of the means of production, the bourgeoisie, and participate only marginally in the fruits of their labour. As producers of surplus value, they create the basis of national wealth, yet their living conditions are frequently precarious. The rural proletariat must be included among working-class writers. Small farmers are a peripheral group of the rural proletariat, who often hardly exist above subsistence level, while contributing to the national wealth. Equally peripheral to the working class are the rising number of people in precarious employment, and the unemployed.

Today, people working in formerly middle-income jobs find themselves increasingly on short-term contracts, low pay, precarious working and living conditions, and the gulf between the haves and have-nots is growing. For this reason, we felt it to be in keeping with our understanding of second culture that all poets who identified with the condition of the working class, who share in this experience and articulate it, should be part of our project.

We tried to reach out to as many poets in Ireland as possible by using word of mouth, trade union and poetry networks. The contributors collected here represent the span of generations, women and men, North and South of the island, writing in Irish and English, from rural and urban backgrounds. In order to highlight the poets' connection with the working-class experience, we have included for each contributor a short biography. All writers focus on themes that are meaningful to working-class communities and write about them from their individual perspectives. These include class, the treatment of women, employment conditions, unemployment, poverty, violence, the environment, homelessness, emigration, immigration, prejudice, racism, clerical abuse, addiction, mental health issues, and dependency on social services. Several poems express the sentiments of solidarity and internationalism, and some reflect on very personal life experiences, such as suicide or miscarriage. These are poems about lives lived on the margins.

It is with this experience in mind that the title for this anthology was chosen. The phrase is instantly recognisable in Ireland, but may need explanation elsewhere. It comes from the *Proclamation of the Republic,* issued at the time of the 1916 Easter Rising, Ireland's attempt to free herself from British rule. In it the Provisional Government solemnly pledges to the people of Ireland that

The Republic guarantees religious and civil liberty, equal rights and equal opportunities to all its citizens, and declares its resolve to pursue the happiness and prosperity of the whole nation and of all its parts, cherishing all the children of the nation equally.

This oath, we feel, has not been fulfilled. The poems contained in the volume bear witness to this.

However, the Irish Swiftian tradition ensures that readers will find the poems entertaining as well as thought provoking, and there is a great variety and range in voices and styles. In relation to the forms, there is a trend, also reflected in this collection, towards more song/rap/performance poetry—a reminder perhaps that the origins behind the word lyric is poetry accompanied by a lyre. More recently, Bob Dylan received the Nobel Prize for Literature for his song lyrics. As Brecht commented in another context, *"If (Shelley's) great ballad 'The Mask of Anarchy', written immediately after the bloody upheaval in Manchester (1819), suppressed by the bourgeoisie, does not correspond to the common description of realist writing, we must ensure that the definition of realist writing is changed, expanded, and made more comprehensive."* New expression generates new forms and writers must not feel enslaved by the old.

We are deeply grateful to the Irish Trade Union Movement for the solidarity shown for this publication, as expressed in the financial support by Fórsa, UNITE, CWU, Mandate, the Belfast and Galway Trades Councils. We also thank the poets for the windows into their lives. These are voices that matter, that need to be heard.

Galway, August 2019

Contents

Gary Allen

was born into a large working-class family in Ballymena. When he left school, he worked in local factories before going abroad, living and working in Holland for some time. For the last twenty years, he has been working as a security guard to give himself the time to write. He has published eighteen books of poetry, most recently the long poem, *Sour Hill*, in London. His poems have been published widely in literary magazines including *Irish Pages, Poetry Ireland, London Magazine, The New Statesman, The Poetry Review*, etc.

Cock Robin

I am lying in the back bedroom of my aunt's house
I am pretending to be dead
the roller blind is pulled down, the way it is done

my aunt does not know I am dead
it is wash day
she is throwing soapy water out across the cobbles

my mother does not know yet that she has lost a son
laughing with the other fat girls on the chicken production line
their arms covered in bloody viscus
Funny, she thinks, how death is like birth

the boys in my class, even those who dislike me
and the solemn teachers too
will follow in lines behind my coffin
down familiar streets I hate

and then my father will sigh and pull apart the curtains
too soon

but my heart still beats too loudly
and I am stiff from lying in the same position

the pigeons will not be silent
the sunlight is a constant in the room
and none of them will know what could have been lost.

Fifth Avenue

My father is lost, though he doesn't have the sense of it
rooted to the spot in the subway on Fifth Avenue
listening to a half-wit badly singing Danny Boy

he is stinking of flea-pits and fortified wine
this is the smell of the corpses decomposing
on the escalators taking them up to Fifth Avenue
to the piled slush and the burst water hydrants

though they have no business at this time of the day
on Fifth Avenue among Tiffany and Abercrombie & Fitch

in ten years my father got no farther than downtown Bronx
at first he stayed away from the Irish pub on the corner of 445W & 238th St
but everything is themed

my father doesn't read books
he likes the horses
he doesn't make friends easy
like small talk in diners over eggs and coffee

and Danny Boy has eyes turned in, like his toes
a reel to reel that keeps starting over —

my father doesn't speak the language
the street signs are mostly numbers
the Irish are the wrong type of Irish

and my father was never in New York in his own lifetime
though he thought Cagney the business.

Joseph Allen

is the brother of Gary Allen. He left school at sixteen, studied for O levels but did not sit the exams. He did an apprenticeship in painting and decorating, then worked as a skilled labourer, and is currently employed as a security guard at a local government building. He plays gigs as a Delta blues guitarist/singer harmonica player. Joseph Allen has published seven books of poetry.

Obituaries

No expectations for the boy
eating cold toast
in the church schoolroom
shirt sleeves buttoned down

a house built on
chairs of frustration
like barricaded towns

days of bored teachers
an education leading to boring jobs

reading the obituaries
of a generation
among examination results

retirements strung out in shopping centres
hospital appointments
and cranberry sandwiches
drowning in a wave
or aimless dog walks
clinging on.

Anne Mac Darby-Beck

was born into a working-class family in rural County Laois. When she left school, she worked in a factory until being made redundant. She moved to Kilkenny, married a tradesman and had a child. After working in various jobs over the years, she now works for the local authority. She wrote extensively as a child but fell away from the practice in her late teens. She joined a women's study group in a local village, which morphed into a writers' group. With the encouragement of the group, she began to write again. She writes poems and short stories in her free time outside of work and home. Her poems and stories have been published in various anthologies and magazines such as *Cyphers, Poetry Ireland Review, Crannog, Skylight 47*, "*1916-2016 Anthology of Reactions*", *A New Ulster*, etc. She won a first place in Syllables Poetry Competition.

Chlorophyll

Heavy steps on the stairs
to the grimy canteen,
garish orange notice
warns against borrowing
from the newspaper stand.

Heave the skylight open,
release the smoky air;
groan into a plastic chair
too tired to eat.

Must use these spare minutes,
to write something down;
distracted by the intercom,
chatter in the room.

Through the open skylight
on the cool air
from a beech tree comes
soft shower of leaves.

One lands on a half-filled page
life dried from the veins —
but around the edges
there are still a few specks
of chlorophyll.

Patrick Bolger

is a writer and visual artist. His poetry gives voice to issues often silenced and marginalised in Irish society—including childhood sexual violence and the corrosive impact that childhood trauma, when met with silence at a familial, community and societal level, can have on both the individual and the collective. It explores themes of self-identity, addiction, mental health, masculinity, love and relationships. Born into a working-class family in rural County Wicklow, Patrick was the first in his family to attend college. Social justice and the role of privilege in creating class divisions and prejudices in society are also explored in his work.

We are All Beasts

They come in their hundreds.
Men of the northwest
And the occasional woman

Bringing their animals with them
From Kiltimagh and Bohola
From Turlough and Breaffy
To the livestock mart in Balla.

There's trade to be done,
No sentiment in selling.

The beasts are spat from trailers
All lost legs and confusion
Many have never left home before

And the farmers are all business
Slapping stickers to their backs
Not names but numbers
A very male goodbye

When all the paperwork is done
They take smoke and strong tea
Before entering the ring
Where they gather
In a half circle of trust

Standing together
Legs against legs
Arms around each other
They are a sauna of farmers

Free from the solitude and stillness
Of their everyday

The chatter and nod of heads
The finger circling and cutting the air
The shoulder squeeze of approval
For a good price

They wouldn't stand at the bar
This close
They wouldn't embrace on the sideline
Or in church at Sunday mass

But here
In selling ring number 1
On this May morning
In the livestock mart in Balla
In the county of Mayo

Farming men
With pitted nails
And sun-dried faces
Wrap strong arms around the other
And feel the heat
And the fear
And the dread

Of going home
Of never going home

We are all beasts.

Goin Homeless

I

they're goin homeless
it's the latest trend
in a country on its knees
they're goin homeless

it's a bit like the Macarena
In the 1990s

young girls, teenage mothers
skipping hand in hand
into the homeless office
to go homeless

the needle marks hidden
beneath their skinny jeans

they're goin homeless
like their ma's before them

when you grow up darlin
I'm goin to teach you how to be homeless

in my day you had to wait for a house

now youse have it so easy

go homeless
tell them you're goin homeless
they'll let you self-accommodate

you'll get to stay in a hotel every night
(well until there's a big concert or match on)
then you'll have to find somewhere else to go

next it will be the hubs
dress up for the party

Free Food
Free Rent

a step up from the hotels you can say
they used to let you stay 6 months
but you might get two years now.

two years of free food.
why don't we all go homeless?
in one big group.

after two years you might get a house
maybe old Mrs. Keane up the road will die
and you can get her house
don't mind what the fuckin neighbours think

II

fuckin spongers, goin homeless,
plannin and plottin
to go homeless
hatchin plans over skinny cappuccinos
in the Square,
affidavits stuck in their skinny ass pockets

we hear you, skanky bitches
with your squealing brats
goin homeless

spendin your children's allowance in H&M

dressin up to go homeless
do you dress up to piss us off?

we open late and close early
does that piss you off?
sometimes we just decide
fuck it
we won't self-accommodate anybody

what a laugh we had that Friday afternoon!

that'll fuckin teach them
to go homeless

young girls, teenage mothers
skipping hand in hand
into the homeless office
to go homeless

the needle marks hidden
beneath their skinny jeans

III

I'm not goin homeless
I'm goin mad
I love her bones
me little baba
but when she cries
at night

me head rattles,
me ma screamin at me
to make her stop screamin
and me screamin at her to
stop screamin at me

me head rattles

me head is fucked
I drop one
then two

I wake up
to more screamin
me ma
me baba
me

screamin
I don't see the needle marks
on me legs
as I pull on me jeans

I dress the baba in the latest
All pink and fluffy

me ma screamin
that she wants me out
and the baba
out
me screamin back
the baba screamin
me ma screamin
the baba cryin
the baba frightened

you're scarin her ma
fuck it ma
you're scarin her
we're goin
we're goin homeless

the door rattling off its hinges
the stupid bitch

Evidence

Those damn boys. Occasions of sin.
He once told me. Cardinal Desmond Connell,
prince of the roman catholic church.
He nodded, leaned his head to one
side and tried to hold my hand.
He was sorry. He said.
At the age of 31, I sat alone in
the High Court of Ireland. On a leather
seat, dark wood, the skin around my nails

bleeding. I sat. Waiting. For the offer.
On this settling day.
I was assured that my voice, would never
be heard by the High Court of Ireland.
In the absence of compassion and
apologies, they bring forth money.
Trading in their own currency. The roman catholic church.
Where my bitten nails sit, I shake.
The offer is put to me, I should
accept, I am told as they will never go
higher, without proof of penetration.
Without proof of penetration.
The eight year old boy, me 23 years
before this day, should have collected
evidence. Evidence. My blood. Or his.
Semen.

Blessed are those who have not
seen and yet believe.

This is the Roman Catholic Church
This is the institution that moved Thomas Naughton
Of the Kilteagan fathers
From Africa to the West Indies
From the West Indies to Aughrim Street
From Aughrim Street to Valleymount
From Valleymount to Donnycarney
From Donnycarney (via Stroud) to Ringsend.

(Stroud was a spiritual therapy facility for paedophile clergy)

This is the institution that wanted
'Proof of Penetration'

Evidence.

Sara Boyce

is from a small coastal village in Donegal but now lives in working-class West Belfast. She works with the Participation and Practice of Rights project, a human rights organisation that works with marginalised communities, building power to exact accountability and transparency from the state. Since the 1980s, Sara has been active in campaigns north and south of the border, on issues such as anti-racism, the environment, language and women's rights. Sara's poetry in turn is informed by this activism. She believes in the potential of poetry to give voice to people's real struggles against inequality and oppression in all its forms, and in the right of every individual to live a life of dignity and fulfilment.

What Doesn't Kill You

I know time has changed me
but hope to still be recognised,
I keep my hair cropped short,
a nod to the bad old days,
my back now fairly hunched —
the burden of folk memory;
buckshot and brass medals
have made a pin cushion of my chest
so that when I draw breath
The Croppy Boy whistles through.

I splash my face with bog water
its metal tang awakening my tongue,
shake out my *cóta mór*,
downcast through lack of wear,
 edge my awkward elbows into sleeves
inhale its acerbic odour,
pleased to catch a faint trace of its
'you'll not own me' attitude.

Once more I broach the cobbled city
bereft now of the clatter of hooves
that continuous clipping that attended
the birth of our new language, with
its loan words from the French —
Liberté, Egalité, Fraternité.

****

I listen to the slip and slide of boardroom babble,
worry that I don't speak this newer lingo
of outsourcing and efficiency,
customers and zero hours,
skivers and early risers
of illegal human beings.

I rub my thumb over the notches
of the *bata scoir* around my neck ,
touch scar tissue formed by
knotted ropes and sally rods;
this ill-fitting argot
provokes phantom pains —
the memory of a higher code,
still carried downwind from Cave Hill;
I straighten my shoulders and know
I needn't worry about being recognised.

Its Beating Heart

'Live in the heart of the city' the outsize banner proclaims.

Its dirty disposable heart,
strewn with coffee cups in latte coloured puddles,
where bicycle wheels, bent like Uri Geller spoons,
muffle lampposts on street corners softened
with smoke from a nearby bingo hall,
where hopeful hearts quicken then slow,
as the two fat ladies wave from the opposite side of the hall.

'Live in the heart of the city'.

Its swollen imperial heart,
whose arteries still pulse a royal blue,

and watch its newcomer families
gather in safety knots within the folds
of the Famine Queen's marbled frock
and wonder —
would she be as *flaithiúil* with her fivers*
for those foodbanks they depend on?

'*Live in the heart of the city*'.

Its brick-bled and rain-wept heart,
whose municipal vision cuts through
its public benches;
no space here for homeless bums
Meanwhile, down a high street entry
great black-backed gulls
span a crumpled sleeping bag
in search of carrion.

[*the English translation of the Irish word *flaithiúil* is *generous*. Queen Victoria,
known as the Famine Queen, is reported to have donated £5 to the Irish Famine
Relief Fund. On the same day she donated a fiver to the Battersea Cats and Dogs
Home.]

Kathy's Tree

New to this parish,
her suitcase still unpacked,
she plugged in the phone
and rang the City Hall.

Her name and address duly declared
 his irked sigh lopped her words
Complaint form's in the post; tick the relevant box —
dampness, leaks, whatever, post it back,
saw toothed sharp, she bit back
Is there a box on your form for 'No trees'?

Silence sliced through the line;
she spoke slowly, like he'd come down its river in a bubble
There are no trees on Danube Street,
her Mancunian lilt lighting up each vowel.

She heard him turn the pages of his playbook:
I don't think that's our Department
I'm not sure that those houses come with trees
The roots can cause structural damage
Trees attract anti-social elements —
pigeons, starlings, unruly children...

Now she chopped him off like a dead branch,
I've walked up the Antrim Road,
the leafy Antrim Road, BT15,
two and a half miles from Danube Street,
how are people meant to breathe, to live?

She scanned the dispirited streetscape
from her sitting room window,
eyes tracing out the concrete lines
that criss-crossed the pavement,
before resting on the sunlit sign —

Danube Street BT13.

The brightness illuminated her mind's eye
and she was once more back in Manchester,
lying in the shade of its black poplars
cramming for her geography O levels.

Facts coursed through her teenage brain —

the Danube's a lifeline that flows
from Black Forest to Black Sea
through corridors of cherry,
groves of willow and oak tree.

She wondered if he'd passed his O Levels,
if he knew where the Danube was;
she wondered if it was any easier to breathe
beyond the barricade, over on the Falls.

Kathy replaced the receiver,
and slowly opened her suitcase,
the scent of balsam infusing the air,
reminding her to breathe,
in and out, in and out.

David Butler

works as a full-time writer. As this does not entitle him to unemployment benefit, he makes ends meet by teaching courses in creative writing. Over the years, he worked in quite a number of different positions—waiter, barman, factory-hand, doorman, hotel-porter, gardener, chef, tutor. His second poetry collection, *All the Barbaric Glass*, was published by Doire Press in 2017. His 11 poem cycle 'Blackrock Sequence', a Per Cent Arts Commission which was illustrated by his brother, Jim, was winner of the World Illustrators Award (books, professional section) 2018. The impetus for 'Dockers, 1930' came from his having attended Lee Coffey's excellent 'In Our Veins' in the *Peacock* in early 2019. 'Dockers, 1930' was first published in the *Poets meet Politics* competition anthology (June 2019).

Dockers, 1930

First light.
The descent from the tenements.
Flat-caps and donkey-jackets, shoulders
hunched against an easterly would skin you.
Keen-eyed, skint, eager for the scrimmage about
the rough pulpit to catch 'the read', the foreman
meting out who works, who idles.
A hard graft for the chosen.
Scant light
aslant through moiling
dust inside the dusky hold of a collier
where rope-muscled, calloused hands
rough-handle shovel-hafts, scraping, angling,
hacking irascible black-flecked phlegm until,
begrimed like pantomime blackamoors, they emerge
to carry their thirst like a wage and pay out
the bitter tithe — the match-boxed shilling
that buys the wink and nod.
It's that or starve.

Peggie Caldwell

is originally from Donegal but has lived in Dublin for over 10 years. She grew up in a rural working-class home where they were taught the importance of hard work and the value of education. She is a teacher and like so many people from rural Ireland (past and present) leaving for her was the only way she could get that education and ultimately get a job. She emigrated to Scotland and lived there for several years before returning to Dublin. Dublin has become her home now, but Donegal will always have her heart. Rural Ireland, particularly Donegal, has been neglected by successive governments in terms of jobs, investment and infrastructure. Peggie's poems reflect her attitude towards the inequalities that exist in our healthcare system, the impact emigration has on communities, and how ultimately Ireland, for all her protestations, is a class-based society. She lives in hope that we can do better for everyone.

Take a Number

I never noticed the tangled web before
Traversing corridors, hallways, up doors.
Blue, green, red, all leading someplace:
Someplace different to here;
Someplace better than here.

I see her come to the desk,
Be directed, politely, to follow blue,
All the way to the end and take a seat.
She won't be back to join us
In this never-ending waiting queue.

The receptionist sounds different —
I hear this and look up.
She scowls at the man who comes in
With a pain in his chest: How long is the wait?
Please take a number and it will be called.

Still They Go

The wains still go, shattering hearts,
against this alluring landscape of neglect.

No rollercoaster joyride spin down the road —
dreaming of living, never living the dream.

Barren fields, once bartered sunsets, now deal
famine roads, fragmented roads, forsaken roads.

How do they get on track when the tracks
were never laid in this stony mournful ground?

Fallacies echo:
Live Register lowest it's been since 2008.

But in these hills the white noise rebounds,
the absence of fledgling song deafening us.

I See You Too

When I tell them I left school at thirteen,
Took the boat at sixteen then came back again
They think they know me, that they've seen me before.
Eyes narrow, inspecting cratered hands that wear,
Like gloves, the tapestry of my hard luck story.

I see it in their put-on pauses and plastic faces
That they think they've heard it all before:
That they can read my dog-eared pages
Without opening the book —
Know how my story begins,
Know how my story ends.

They find me curious, my ayes and naws,
And think it strange that I should question them.
What school did you go to? no longer shames me —
Baptising backroads and townlands, they lose their way.
Lose interest — never had an interest.
Silver spooned, setting down markers
To hold their place — put me in my place.

They say it's my shoulders carrying heavy loads,
That they have opened all the doors.
Except the locked door into their manicured lives
Where I do not belong with my broken
And dirty nails that scrub and bleach their floors.

Lorraine Carey

has had poetry her published in *Poetry Ireland Review, Orbis, Poethead, Prole, Smithereens, The Ogham Stone, Constellate, Abridged, The Curlew* and many others. A Pushcart Prize nominee, her art has also featured in several journals including *Skylight 47* and *North West Words*. Many of her poems reflect her own and others' experiences of emigration, unemployment, exclusion, the stigma concerning mental ill health struggles and marginalisation in society. Her poems have featured on The Christmas Poetry Programme on RTE Radio 1 and local radio. A contributor to several anthologies, her debut collection is *From Doll House Windows* (Revival Press). A version of 'Lonely Bones' was published on *I Am Not A Silent Poet*, April 2018, and 'Checkpoint, Culmore 1980' was published in *Epoque Press*, April 2018.

Checkpoint, Culmore 1980

We tumbled into Gran's Fiesta
on Fridays after school,
until we got the Renault 5.
A straight run through, Moville, Redcastle,
Quigley's Point, Muff, then border territory
and much better roads
beyond Customs on the bend.
Mother eased her foot off the floor
approaching Culmore.
As the ramps came into view,
her heartbeats mirrored
the checkpoint's flashing.
Told us to sit still, as we giggled
and stared at shiny rifles with triggers of steel.
Wound down her window to a babyfaced soldier
his soft contoured chin, yet to meet a razor.

He peered in and winked, smiled at us in the back,
she hoped to bypass the search bay and torchlight beams.
Green berets sat, looked silly on their teenage heads,
guns slung over slender shoulders.
Prayed they wouldn't peer too closely
at the photo, or at her and Gran.
The dark night cast welcome shadows.
They shared dyed black curls

and frantic fidgets, almond eyes and nervous smiles.
She wound the window up, shut out the frosty night
with a sigh, waved goodbye to other mothers' sons.

Placed Gran's licence in the sun visor's flap,
thankful for the resemblance.
Relaxed she drove on, indicated right
down Greenhaw Road, into Superfare's car park.
Picked up bargains and exchanged grumbles
about the pound, sterling shopping, border hopping,
evenings of memories
with her late mother.

Lonely Bones

London's Eye can see into your soul,
the metal mammoth a fixture
of your lifetime. Gathering at fountains
on Saturday nights, clutching at camaraderie
with forced fervour, weekend drunk and lonely.
The brown envelope's leftovers hinge on a Soho visit,
strip club or a jostle in your local, as Cockneys harp
about market stall trends,
or Arsenal, or Everton,
whatever.
Misplacing accents as you swallow your own,
toning it down when all you crave
is to belong.

You miss the incessant screech
of herring gulls, squabbling at the dock,
the chug of trawlers, loaded to the scuppers.
Netted bowels heaving with their silvery catch.
Scales like glints off a blade,
shimmering in rays.
Betty from two doors down,
proffers the only net you'll see now,

cushioning the sparse wisps of her blue rinse.
Smells smash into you, street scents raid your senses.
Your memory bank at odds with dillisk and sea salt,
thick on a sticky breeze.
The tube station hell, midlife
and monotony herded up escalators,
anonymity in headphones
and at war with you.

No twitching curtains
no shop counter reports
of the recently deceased,
no weather forecasts delivered with gusto.
Instead, the apparitions flit by
at dusk and dawn, shadows floating
with jangled keys, lunged in the lock,
turning goodnight on the world.

Aidan Casey

was born in Dublin in and did a B.A. in English and Philosophy at University College Dublin. He emigrated from Ireland in the eighties and since then he has been teaching English in Spain, Germany and Ireland as well as writing code for websites and developing apps for mobile devices.

Dog in the Manger

Tell us your tale of a dog,
the wrong bitch, just enough selfregard
to drag you away, tail between your legs,
no longer one of us, prickly as a hedgehog
and more outofcharacter than in,
till the years are streets without lampposts or corners
and you can hardly remember who you are.

Like a country shaking off English rule,
you scrambled ashore from a sea of misfortune.
The jobs went away to a coolie economy,
he was fed up, she needed a wage, an abortion
and a month out turned into a year.
You'd have gone back then if you'd had the fare.
Now you can hardly remember who you are.

Who'd know you now with your stake in the country,
bitching about wogs at the cheese and wine evening,
whose people went howling as often as ragged
to beg on the boreens half savage with hunger,
with your golf club, your iPhone, your Indo on Sunday,
you're the dog in the manger and no fear
you will ever remember who you are.

Anne Casey

Originally from Clare, Anne Casey spent several years in Dublin before emigrating to Australia. She has worked as a kitchen hand, bar worker, restaurant server, factory packer, shop assistant, journalist and editor. Over the past 25+ years, Anne has written on workers' rights, workplace discrimination, and on gender, environmental, humanitarian and socio-political issues. Anne's protest poetry has been widely published internationally; she passionately believes in the power of words to effect change. Her ecopolitical poem 'Recipe for a Giant Pickle' was selected for performance by international environmental activists, the Climate Guardians at the Biennale of Australian Art 2018, the largest ever showcase of Australian artists. Her second poetry collection, *out of emptied cups* (Salmon Poetry 2019) interrogates the intersection between body and life experience, particularly as this relates to women and bodily autonomy. Anne has won/been shortlisted for poetry awards in Ireland, Northern Ireland, the USA, the UK, Canada and Australia. The poem 'after the commission' was first published in *HUSK* magazine Issue 6 in August 2018, and subsequently in *out of emptied cups*.

after the commission

a waft of smouldering candle grease
laced with a trace of incense
the sharp slap of flat soles
on a marble floor
dark shapes filter past one by one
spectres reflecting on polished brass

Let us begin with a prayer
a rosary catches on a sharp edge
spilling shiny
Our Fathers, Hail Marys
and Glory Bes
between uneasy feet

doves cross to and fro
beyond yawning windows
a distant boom
silver tongues slick down old panes
glossing over transparency
light leaves the room

under the same clouds
a mother looking down
holds her dying son
the sodden air stirring
with a sudden chill
in some dark corner
a child is crying still

Michael Casey

has published five novels, a book of non-fiction and an award-winning chapbook of short stories. Six of his plays have been produced by the Umbrella Theatre Company—one, by invitation, in the Henrik Ibsen Museum, Oslo. In his writings, he has advocated the 'share economy' in which the distinction between workers and owners would disappear. He has also written in support of a Tobin tax on financial transactions.

No Room at Home

Five-thirty, still dark, aching cold.
Snores and hawks of a hundred men,
waking sick and chilled to the bone.
Pull on boots, stand freezing
on the corner, look as strong as you can,
like a horse or at least a pony
to impress the Ganger Man.

He comes at six, looking for ten skins,
looks you up and down, walks on to judge
the rest of the line; fear spurs on
the heart until he returns, sizes up again,
notices the boots caked in fresh cement.
He jerks his thumb again to-day.
Thank God for the Ganger Man.

Ten skins pile into the back of the van
and vie for space between diesel drums,
barrows, shovels and concrete blocks.
God knows where the site will be
but you will have a fiver in your pocket
by nightfall, if you survive the day;
all thanks to the Ganger Man.

You remember the pulse-beat of the ship
as it eased away from the harbour wall,
turned slowly in churning water
and headed out to open sea,
spires and houses fading into mist.
That was how the journey began
that brought you to the Ganger Man.

You'll never have a roof or kitchen
like they have at home. Soon
you won't even have a hostel bed.
You'll sleep on the street and hope
not to wake in the morning; the day
will dawn when you get your wish
and become an also-ran, one skin less,
one horse less for the Ganger man.

Rachel Coventry

grew up in a council estate in Dunfermline, misspent her youth in Hackney and now lives in Galway where she wonders if her there will be another contract in September. Her debut collection, *Afternoon Drinking in The Jolly Butchers*, is published by Salmon Poetry.

Night Bus

We are up against it now
now that the end has become
comprehensible. I remember

when it wasn't. Do you recall
driving over that hill into Mega-City One?
Like young love, the future is over.

The question now is how much
will it cost to keep the teeth in my head
till the end? How much will it cost

to keep my teeth in till I'm lowered
to my final resting place in a corner
of Rahoon Cemetery?

Men are like buses. There will always be
another but I haven't really committed to walking
till I've gone too far to run back to the stop.

Once I'm that far gone, I must contend
with the fact it may pass me, its passengers
held together in the light;

its passengers held together in the static
of being randomly assigned to this particular journey
with nothing to do but ignore each other stoically.

Even so, I will be alone out here
out here with the ghosts of wolves
and rapists still in their flesh. I will be jealous.

Once you told me you were beaten up
and how after a while the punches no longer hurt
they just felt like air moving.

Billy Craven

moved back to Ireland in 2015 after spending the best part of a decade living and working abroad. Since then, he has been teaching in secondary schools on short-term contracts, resulting in precarious employment and living conditions. He sees traditionally well-paid, secure employees being driven into a poverty trap and a State which has somehow convinced people that this is as good as they can expect. Lurching from crisis to crisis, those responsible simply brazen it out, wait for the media to lose interest and then carry on regardless, with very little consequence or accountability and no effective opposition from their peers.

Ireland's Having a Boom

No mortgage and increasing rents
(Ireland's having a boom)
People living in the Park in tents
(And Ireland's having a boom)

A million patients on a waiting list
(While Ireland's having a boom)
Can't tell if it's cancer or just a cyst
(But Ireland's having a boom)

No money for our education
(Ireland's having a boom)
No chance of pay scale restoration
(But Ireland's having a boom)

More platitudes from politicians
(Ireland must be having a boom)
2 years in a month's direct provision
(Yet Ireland's having a boom)

We've babies entombed in septic tanks
And money tied up in septic banks
And GDP that insists we're wealthy
But to me those numbers don't look too healthy

Coz I've got no mortgage and increasing rents
(But Ireland's having a boom)
They're snorting lines inside the gents
(Ireland must be having a boom)

We lap it up and insist we're great
(Ireland's having a boom)
Coz we passed gay marriage and repealed the 8th
(And Ireland's having a boom)

So why do I have to emigrate?
(If Ireland's having a boom)
Regret I left it quite so late
(Yet Ireland's having a boom)

Good times are back, so quench your thirst
(Coz Ireland's having a boom)
Think I just heard a bubble burst
Ireland's having a boom

Gráinne Daly

lives in Tallaght, Dublin. Educated in Firhouse Community College, she worked in a local chipper and subsequently Dunnes Stores to pay her way through college. After many years of working as a personal assistant, her role was made redundant and she began to focus on her life's passion: writing. She won the UCD Maeve Binchy Award 2019 and was runner-up in the Limnisa Short Story Competition 2019. Her work was highly commended in the Blue Nib Poetry Chapbook Competition 2018 and shortlisted for the Gregory O'Donoghue and Anthony Cronin Poetry Prizes. She has been published in numerous publications such as *Southword Magazine, Dodging the Rain, Ogham Stone* and *Boyne Berries*. Her non-fiction has recently appeared in *The Blue Nib Journal*.

In the shadow of a Dunnes man

Dunnes doorway bleached morning
and night to expunge the scent of
life and street people who limp from
hostel to hovel for a ceiling to shield
the rain, pain, the bleached promises,
solution to shift around the corner
to the Goods In door of a plate glass store
the stable of Bethlehem in Little Ship Street

Emer Davis

was born in Dublin in 1966 and grew up on Achill Island. She emigrated to London in 1990 where she worked for Boots the Chemist for six years. In 2001, she joined the Civil Service and was a member of the PSEU branch committee and for one year was the branch secretary for the Department of Justice, where she campaigned for the atypical workers in the Department to be given permanent contracts in the civil service. She firmly believes in workers' and human rights, and this has been a theme of her poetry. She worked for a month on the EU Relocation Programme on Lesvos Island in January 2016 and this experience inspired her to write many poems about the plight of migrants. In 2018 she moved to New Delhi for work. Several of her poems have been published in Ireland, UK, USA and UAE. 'The Whistleblower' was inspired from a line from Ibsen's play *An Enemy of the People* —'The majority is never right'.

The Whistleblower

Silently
I watch the water
ebb away,
mist washing over me
as I watch
the waves crackle
in the evening sun.

Silently
I stand alone
shunned
from society
for speaking the truth,
silenced by their venom
I stand alone,
and watch the white ripples
cascade across the open sea

Patrick Deeley

was born in rural East Galway in 1953. His mother ran a small family farm and his father was a carpenter and hurley maker. After training as a primary teacher, Patrick worked for many years in a school in Ballyfermot. His poems have appeared widely in leading literary magazines and anthologies in Ireland and abroad over the past four decades. Patrick writes books for children, published by O'Brien Press, including *The Lost Orchard*, winner of the Eilis Dillon and Bisto awards. His bestselling memoir, *The Hurley Maker's Son* (Transworld) was shortlisted for the 2016 Irish Book of the Year Award. His poetry awards include the 2014 Dermot Healy International Poetry Prize and the US-based Lawrence O'Shaughnessy Award for 2019. 'Clearance' was originally published in *Rochford Street Review* (Australia) and 'Another Life' in *Prole* (UK) and in his seventh collection *The End of the World* (Dedalus Press, 2019).

Clearance

Budless, stripped of leafage and bark, trees sizzle and tick,
become mewling animals —
with smouldering hoofs, with cauterised antlers
puffing smoke as they lean away from us

into fire-blistered distance. Become
charcoal effigies. Bits of them flake off, or momentarily flap
ashy winglets before collapsing.
Or they crack explosively apart, trunks grinning

red-grained and open, while what pass
for their crowns —fused, shrunken—
crookedly slide and tumble. It takes days for the clearance
to cool. The farmer who owns the wood

appears and disappears, mumbling
about how the land is forever, the land is his. Shrugs
at the good riddance of scrub. Meaning
willow and hazel that spar in dens,

nests, horizontal understoreys. Meaning
tall, pliant poplar, and aspen, the long-stemmed whisperer.
Meaning pine and beech, elm
and oak. The forester, shy in face of all,

asks us to save what is saveable. Velvety dust
squeaks, smears and sears.
Our chainsaws hop off the heat-toughened trunks. We turn
back when rain runs everything

into a morass. There will be growth again — lichens,
hummocks of moss, raddled foundations
open to fern and foxglove. Blackbirds
will swear their liquid oaths, spiders build. Some other April

will find a living wilderness here, incineration
covered over as if it had never happened.
We stare at the ground
and tell ourselves the only blaze will be of furze blossoming.

Another Life

He's here, the chilly air fringing his grouchiness.
"Thirty years," he says, "hauling coal."
Enough to wear the heart, and the fireplace, out.

You clear a path for him in his stooped blunder
through the house, the wind funnelling
and every photo and figurine threatening take-off.

Bag after bag he empties with a flurried
thrum into the sooty bin — compacted "nuggets",
"gems" the shape and size of goose eggs.

You pick one up. It feels silken to your fingertips,
yet induces an itch. Its metallic gleam
suggests a meteoroid fire-balling through space.

But you dream the ancient subterraneum
of which it formed part, forests flooded and sunken,
made to simmer in vast, shallow lakes.

Peat, lignite, coal coming about. No help found
in the slow burn of regret if now, again,
forests must drown, the land be over-swept.

"Thirty years," he reiterates. "I started early, kept
going." You attempt camaraderie, recall
summers you spent doing man-labour too young,

in lost bogs of Killoran and Gleann. The sleán
was an education; the books would carry more weight.
He stands, thin as a waif. His hand shakes

as he drains a glass of orange juice. The whites
of his eyes set against his coal-dust face
look immaculate, say, as a Sunday shirt, another life.

Celia de Fréine

is a multi-genre writer who writes in Irish and English. She was born in Newtownards, County Down and now divides her time between Dublin and Connemara. Her most recent book, *Ceannródaí*, a biography of Louise Gavan Duffy, won ACIS Duais Leabhar Taighde na Bliana (2019) and was nominated on the shortlist for An Post Irish Book Awards (2018). Celia won scholarships to attend secondary school. She studied at night for a BA from UCD and was awarded an MA in Creative Writing from Lancaster University for which she studied while holding down a full-time job and raising five children. 'Stórtha Arda' was first published in *Faoi Chabáistí is Ríonacha* (ClóIar-Chonnacht, 2001); 'Tall Storeys', its English translation was first published in *Scarecrows at Newtownards* (Scotus Press, 2005).

Stórtha Arda

Tá áthas ar Aingeal gur chuimhnigh sí ar a lapaí.
Agus is mór an áis di freisin, a culaith chait dhubh.
I dtosach bíonn imní uirthi eitilt róghar
don ghealach ar eagla go ndiúgfaí a cuid fola.
Is rud amháin é eitilt le linn taibhrimh —
ar an saol seo is gá iarracht níos déine a dhéanamh.

Dein dearmad ar mheáchan do choirp,
a deir sí, léi féin. *Sín amach do ghéaga*
ar nós curaidh céad méadar snámh brollaigh.
B'fhéidir gurb é seo an t-aon seans a gheobhas tú.
Ní theastaíonn uait fás suas i sluma,
fiche stór in airde. Gan chrainn. Gan jab.

Le héirí na gréine gabhann thar abhainn,
is tugann faoi deara dallóga liathdhearga
ag bolgadh as díonteach. *Caith do shúil*
thairis sin, a mholann di féin. Laistigh
stacaí leabhar, dealbha ón Oirthear.
Is ón urlár mailpe, croitheann a scáth chuici.

Tall Storeys

Angela is glad she remembered her flippers.
And her black catsuit comes in handy.
At first she is afraid to fly too close
to the moon in case she bleeds.
It's one thing flying in dreams.
In real life it takes a greater effort.

Ignore the weight of your body,
she tells herself. *Arc your arms like*
a hundred metre breaststroke champion.
This may be your only chance.
You don't want to grow up in a slum.
Twenty storeys high. No trees. No job.

Dawn breaks as she crosses the river.
She sees peach curtains billow
from a nearby penthouse.
Take a closer look, she urges.
Inside stacks of books. Oriental sculptures.
From the maple floor her shadow beckons.

Francis Devine

was born in London, and is a retired Tutor, SIPTU College, Dublin. He has published *Organising History: A Centenary of SIPTU, 1909-2009,* and histories of the Communications Workers' Union and the Medical Laboratory Scientists' Association; was an editor of *Saothar, Journal of the Irish Labour History Society;* and, with Steve Byrne & Friends, issued the CD *My Father Told Me* in 2014 with a second CD, *An Ownerless Corner of Earth,* due later in 2019. His poetry collections are *Red Star, Blue Moon* (1997), *May Dancer* (2007) and *Outside Left* (2017). 'Hup Gralton' & 'When Abdul Moneim Khalifa Met Darach Ó Catháin' were first published in *Red Star, Blue Moon* (Elo Publications, Dublin, 1997), 'The Steamship *Hare'* was published in *May Dancer* (Watchword, Dublin, 2007).

The Steamship *Hare*

for Pádraig Yeates

Since first light
we were there,
cramped close against the Manchester
Shed at the South Wall,
a clawing dampness
enveloping the quays,
all eyes sifting the fog,
watching the bar for the first
sign of a heralded deliverance.

The cold slow bore —
worms in a stair skirting —
mother's thin shawleen
insufficient to lag the bones,
the fevered excitement of daybreak
waning, belief in Jim
challenged by rumour, begrudgery
and the citing of false gods.

Then at a quarter to one,
a Port & Docks Board man
high on a steam shovel, glass to eye,
spotted the streaming bunting,
the flutter of the National Transport

Workers' Federation flag,
the steamship *Hare* butting
into Liffey mouth, entering history,
bearing Larkin deep
inside our souls.

There was no disorder
but disciplined attendance,
a silent respect for Brothers
Seddon and Gosling —
important, bowler-hatted Englishmen
from the Trades Union Congress —
a patient vigil rewarded
by ticketed parcels containing
ten pounds of potatoes
and a further ten pounds of bread,
butter, sugar and tea, jam and fish —
all in boxes and bags with the letters
'CWS' printed boldly on the side.
Our mother shared out our ration
with other unfortunates in the building,
something that seemed
unquestionably natural.
There were biscuits for the childer
which we sat on a plate
and would not eat
lest we had nothing
left to admire.

Jim had delivered us from hunger,
now we had to press forward to seize
the Promised Land,
knowing that our army
could henceforth march
on heart *and* belly.
A half century on,
I saw an old, wizeny man
stood outside the GPO on May Day
with the other dribble-drabble few,
cheering Paddy Donegan and Seán Dunne,

a gold, Shilling
Co-operative Society medal
swinging on his grease-shine lapel.
When he told me he got this
for crewing the *Hare*,
I instantly saw his image
in those digital photographs
thousands unconsciously took
on that dank, drear day
in September Nineteen and Thirteen
as evidence that Hope
did once actually walk
amongst us.

Hup Gralton
for Maggie and Packie

Tufted duck raft on the wee lough
below Drumsna, a homeward halt from Sligo.
Melancholic cats sat the half door,
stopped by water boots and cabbage heads,
take neighbours' salutes and enquiries from the stranger.
Mickey, P.A. and Nelson,
their tractor cabs declaring Bree,
munch buttered brack before a summer's turf fire
and puzzle conversations of unfamiliar families,
Dowra, Nicaragua and a charred hall in Effernagh.
We are as cattle in a meadow's oakshade,
yellowhammers crowding bog ash bent behind the wind,
sighing shires barn warm beneath a nebulous red star.
Leaving, I took eight brown, speckled hens' eggs
home for the weans.

A decade ago we stood back agin' McLoughlin's pub.
Across, poor accordion music, honeysuckle and pine sap,
incessant land rails and a vixen banshee,
were snared by bramble chains and muffled lichen green.
You recalled nights with scolding billies,
bacon clods and bread cakes,
whistling vague rendezvous.
Pipe smoke, blue in the fog,
took talk of cattle raids
to the ears of well-wishers,
buried face downwards as gaelic bards on Uist.
After, long letters from New York forgot
bitterness and never stopped loving
a townland to its face or back.

Today, an excited woodcock
rises from a cowslipped hedgerow,
as Kiltubrid Pipers march the throng through Gowel.
Gralton's body is held aloft by a thousand hands
and rooks, frenzied overhead by spring's demand,
fall silent to gaze on red roses

scattered on a dancefloor cleared again of whin.
At that moment half a century's promises
are redeemed in faces where malice is anathema.
Gurranebraher and Willowfield,
Ballyfermot and the Bronx,
mix drinks with Carrick and Dromod,
toasting a defiance of candle and cant,
in sheer exuberance lilt with the year's first swallow:
'Hup Gralton'.

When Abdul Moneim Khalifa Met Darach Ó Catháin

At the wedding,
the swirling, smiling, skirling wedding
of Mohamed-Rashid Ahmed Adan,
Somali Rashid,
and Euridike Eleanora Gschwind,
fair haired Schwäbisch
with her polite fustian clad family,
we celebrated in Meanwood Working Men's
Saturday afternoon Concert Rooms.
Eddie O'Donnell from Black Sod
belted out Basin Street, Quartier Français
Louisiana blasts that got the sweat flowing,
tore the buttons from the stiff, high collar shirts,
got old Aunt Kreszenzia gallivanting with Raouf.
It was wild after that
with mouth and finger music from Bahrain
and Leeds Céilí Band melodeons hitching every
djellabia for unrelenting *Sieges of Ennis*.
Friedemann tunelessly mourned Der Schwarzwald
and Ambrose Aheng Beng hypnotically
stirred downtown Juba with Chicago.

By five o'clock there was a single,
untrammelled market for whatever you're having yourself,
nothing flagged and youth was in excess supply.

Then, from a corner, Darach Ó Catháin sang.
Darach of Leitir Mór
by way of Rath Cáirn and now demolishing,
not quite yet urbanely renewed
Ritter Street off Blackman Lane,
Darach sang and plugged every disparate central
nervous system into some magical maingrid psyche.
No one understood a single word
and everyone understood every word simultaneously.
Abdul Moneim Khalifa,
Comrade Abdul Moneim Khalifa,
Communist poet and Development Economist,
wept at a discovery he thought beyond him.
They embraced, Darach and Abdul Moneim,
the one in dark, Galician dark,
sardines and fulmar eggs Irish,
the other in Nilotic, cardamom coffee,
chilli red Arabaic.
They held hands, entwined their fingers,
called each other brother
and made us all whoop.

Never had there been such a wedding,
the talk tomorrow of Omdurman and Gezira,
Dysart and Ros Muc.
Rashid and Eurid lovingly wrapped
their wonderful wedding present
in the plain, white tissue of their memory
and Wolfgang and Rabah,
Ute and Badria Ibrahim,
each took home a small fragment of the day
in wee ribboned boxes of obligatory,
amoretti flavoured wedding cake.
With the stewards sweeping up,
Darach and Abdul Moneim were still to leave
singing of yellow bitterns and wildebeest.

Eoin Devereux

is from a working-class background and grew up on a council estate in Limerick City. His early interest in punk rock, left-wing politics as well as studying Sociology all raised his awareness of class issues. He is now a Professor of Sociology and class inequalities have been a recurring theme in his academic writing over the last three decades. Eoin writes short fiction and poetry. Homelessness, dementia, the mistreatment of the mentally ill as well as working-class experience have been a focus of his published work to date. His creative writing has been published by the *Irish Times*, broadcast by RTE Radio One and has appeared in journals such as *Southwords, Number Eleven, The Ogham Stone, Boyne Berries, HCE Review and Silver Apples*.

Panthera

Just eight winters old
Hope, my daughter is sleepless
Because of the din
Seeping through the scrubbed pine floorboards
Of tonight's temporary resting place,
A snug hotel room
Big enough to swing an anorexic Tom Cat in

'Tell me another story Mam, from when you were small'

I put down my click-clacking needles
To weave her a familiar yarn
Rehearsing a well-worn tale about my very first storybook
And the cold but dry daffodiled February day
I first held it in my Lilliput hands

'How did you pay for it?'

For one whole year
I saved and saved,
Eight fistfuls of dirty coppers
I planked them in a Chivers jar
In the always night cubbyhole
Under the stairs,
Then I handed them over
To the stout grey cardiganed assistant
In that big bookshop by the bus stop in town

'And you could barely see over the counter'

Yes, I was short-legged for my age
But that didn't stop me from racing home
Leaping across streets, lanes, rows and bows
To devour the strange words
And savour the wild pictures
Scattered across the savannah of every single page
Dangling my feet on the third step of the linoed stairs

'What was it called and what was it all about?'

The Brave Indian Lion,
He lived under the shade of a Banyan Tree
In the Gir Forest
Short of mane, he was known to all, far and near
For his caring nature, his wisdom and kindness
Especially to those who were weaker than him

'Did he help people like us?'

He really cared for people like us,
The roofless
The faceless
The voiceless

He lifted people who'd fallen
He minded people who were broken
He fed people who were hungry
He calmed people who were angry
He was a very very brave Lion in the face of all adversity

My worry-stone words reassure
And, for now, the questions cease
In spite of the Party Conference noise
Under the floorboards
Hope, my daughter drifts
Into a safe harbour of sleep

Cribbing

To be perfectly honest with you
I knew exactly what I was doing
When I swapped places with the Baby Jesus
In the Pro-Cathedral crib

It was just before the sacristan
Bolted the heavy oak doors
To shut out the cold, dark, unforgiving night
I stepped over the low trellis,
Undressed, and hid, crouched, between Mary and Joseph
The red chancel lamp flickered
And slow-danced
On the Jerusalem gold marble altar
But I soon fell asleep

I'd sleep on a clothesline me.

My silent holy sanctuary was short-lived
I was discovered
In the greylight
By the early elderly faithful
Who were horrified
To see a homeless Black Asylum Seeker
Sleeping naked on the hard, straw strewn floor
Of their sacred Christmas crib.

I was quickly shepherded away
Swaddled in a standard issue Garda overcoat (Size 3XL)
Kicking and screaming
Screaming and kicking
To be penned up in the local Bridewell

Handcuffed in the squad car
I was called:

'Nigger',
'Scrounger',
'Waster',
'Madman.'

I met their questions with a wall of silence,
So I was whipped with wet towels,
They left no marks,
But at least I had a bed for the night.

The following morning after a hearty breakfast
An emergency sitting of Dublin District Court heard,
Serious charges concerning Public Order and Trespass,
The priest, sacristan and parishioners told of their distress:

> "We do our bit for the homeless,
> What with our sale of work, soup runs and annual charity ball"

Adding that staple...

> "This is a very quiet community, things like this never happen
> around here."

For my part,
I accepted neither solicitor nor interpreter
Asking instead, to represent myself

The judge asked me if I had anything to say?

Your Honour, I said,

I did this to take a stand against:
The Janus-faced politicians
Who pretend to care
The fire-brigade journalists
Who parachute in, once a year
The vulture banks and speculators
Who prey on the homeless and the poor,

I did this for:
Those hosteled forever in Direct Provision,
Those young mothers on endless housing waiting lists,
Those sleeping in doorways, under bridges, in cars,
Those sleeping in skips, in LIDL tents above in the Phoenix Park,
Those queuing for food parcels,
Those hidden families imprisoned in cheap hotels,
The 198,358 empty dwellings,

Just waiting to be lived in.

Stephen James Douglas

was born into a small working-class family in 1988 and grew up in Maghaberry, Craigavon. The son of a carpet fitter, Stephen worked as his father's apprentice before developing a love for literature at the Royal Belfast Academical Institution. Graduating from The Queen's University, Belfast in 2010 with a joint honours degree in English and Film Studies, Stephen gained a Post Graduate Certificate of Education at Ulster University and has taught in secondary education for seven years. Stephen's poetry has been published in literary magazines including *A New Ulster* and *Automatic Pilot*.

Consumed

A whirlwind generation; we arrived
unannounced with such ferocity
as to deconstruct nature.

Winds of a hundred miles per hour;
We consumed everything in our path —
the path itself.

Left with nothing;
directionless; we consumed each other;
then ourselves, with a ferocity
that made the gods weep.

Tim Dwyer

grew up in Brooklyn above a butcher shop. His parents had emigrated from Galway after WW2. His father worked at an ice cream plant in the South Bronx by day, and as a barman at the corner by night. Tim has an early memory of his father being disabled for months. If not for the landlord, Abe the butcher, suspending the rent, they may have become homeless. The Phil Ochs song often comes to mind, 'There but for fortune go you or I'. Recently retired as a psychologist, Tim was most comfortable working with the poor and working class in public hospitals and prisons. His experiences appear in his poetry and have shaped his writing. His chapbook is *Smithy Of Our Longings: Poems From The Irish Diaspora* from Lapwing Publications and he regularly contributes to Irish literary journals. He recently moved from Connecticut to Bangor, County Down.

Outside the Garden of Remembrance

It could be a cillin, graves for the unborn, unbaptized, beyond sanctified church burial grounds. A small willow tree that crowds pass every day and yet never see. Underneath the umbrella of leaves, a plaque in Irish, likely moved here from a prominent place in the Rotunda. Samhain 1913, formation of a citizen army to protect workers on strike. Samhain, the thin veil between us living and the dead who died in the Dublin Lock Out. As the willow leaves overshadow this plaque, so does this Garden and 1916 overshadow those brutalized and neglected in that long-ago struggle. But right now, also overshadowed, in a curve in the Garden's stone border, in plain view yet overlooked, a grey sleeping bag camouflaged against the foundation. A person is hidden, except for the crown of the head, some strands of red hair. A woman or a man, sleeping in this cillin, what the papers call sleeping rough. It is late morning by the willow tree. Our folklore tells us the willow will take away our sorrows and our sins.

Mike Gallagher

was born on Achill Island in 1941. Like practically all islanders and the majority of young people born on the west coast of Ireland at that time, he was forced to emigrate, arriving in London in 1960. For the next forty years, he worked on building sites there. On returning to Ireland, he worked in construction for a further ten years. He did not find the building industry conducive to writing and, consequently, did not write his first poem until he was sixty-three years old. Since then, he has been published and translated throughout the world. He won the Michael Hartnett Viva Voce competition in 2010 and 2016, was shortlisted for the Hennessy Award in 2011 and won the Desmond O'Grady International Poetry Contest in 2012. In 2018, he was placed at Listowel Writers Week. His poetry collection *Stick on Stone* was published by Revival Press in 2013.

Stick on Stone

We knew each other only as men
Emigration saw to that:
Him in London, me in Achill
Me in London, him in Luton.
Even living together, we remained
Strangers in a rented room,
Speaking, not talking,
Robbed of our relative roles.

Sure, there were memories —
One golden Dukinella day
When Mick the Yank called;
We straddled a low stone wall,
Talked of Wimpy and McAlpine,
Roads and bridges,
Digs and pubs;
The boy was man!

A lunchtime booze in Wandsworth;
Three of us now living in London,
Yet chatting only the once.
Inheritance was split, spoils divided,
Unequally, but with good humour,
Paraic was always his favourite — and mine.

Nights in Castlebar hospital
After the emigrant's dreaded summons:
"Come now, while he still knows you"
Between the awkward silences,
Came words of stuttered support;
And he survived — again and again.

I almost made it, that last time —
Got to Westport before news
Of our final silence.
Now, as I walk in Dromawda,
His gnarled stick, a stolen spoil,
Taps the unsaid
On the tarstone road.

Hi Horse

The empty space behind Bill's hamburger stall,
hard by the brown and blue facade of Elephant
and Castle's Bakerloo Line; the green and the grey
wagons lined up at half past five, drizzle cloying.
The agents barter dead men with their gangers,
then point them to the crush, two hundred strong,
hobnailed, wellingtoned, soleless, sockless, shirtless,
still soaked from the day before, stink of sweat.
Here the gangers are God; you, you, you, wagon four,
miss, miss, you, wagon one, pass, pass, wagon six.
Fix him cold in the eye, do not flinch, stare down
their despair, pass on; you, you're from Kerry, wagon five.
And thus the sons of the poor old woman,
as many leaving as were born, were divided,
three to a bench in the park with a bottle of meths, one
to Harlesden or Heathrow or Hainault, muck shifting,
sewer digging or dragging cables like a Clydesdale,
all going by the handle, Horse, casuals, on the lump,
no tax, no insurance, no compo when maimed,

ten bob for dinner, ten bob at shift's end and ten bob
if you make it tomorrow.
That morning, you stood behind Roscommon Steve,
his broad shoulders curtaining the rising sun one last time.
He got the shift by the Thames in Maidenhead — you didn't.
Thirty bob too high a price, even for this existence.

Paraic and Jack and John

Hardly ten years between them,
the next door neighbours
from that huddle of houses
under Mullach an Árd,
close, too, their destinies,
not too many options there,
the bus up Gowlawám,
the train to Westland Row.
Hollyhead gave them choices:
Preston? Ormskirk? Cricklewood?

Leaving behind

their Dark Rosaleen,
her surplus-to-requirements,
her spalpeen fanachs,
her jilted lovers, cast-offs.
And yet they sang her praises,
her songs of love and hate,
of repression and rebellion
in the Cocks and Crowns and Clarences
of a thousand English towns.

Drilled by

the teachers, the leather-lashing teachers,
no knowledge, no history
imparted here, only know-how,
know how to swing a pick, to wield an axe,

to dig their way through London clay.
Leadógs, twelve of the best, my boys,
now, on your ways, we have no room
for your likes here.

Blessed by

the priests, upholders of the status quo,
apologists for poverty,
for blind obedience,
sex obsessed, the lure of sex,
more sex, less sex, no sex,
fill the pews, fill the plates,
fill the boats, go, spread the word;
your road to heaven
does not leave
from here

Pawns of

politicians, truth's contortionists,
purveyors of false promises,
self-serving hoors,
too busy building dynasties.
No need for you in their grand plans,
more use, you overseas;
so take the boat, the cattle boat,
join the herd.
Prime Beef.

Goodbyes to

the mothers, always the mothers,
the father-mother-farmer mothers,
the savers of hay,
the spreaders of turf;
brought into heat once, maybe twice,
a year, migrant's return, marital duties,
children's allowances, God's word —
stuff like that.

Returning to

the mothers, the dazed, distraught mothers,
in the wake houses, huddled
under Mullach an Árd
after the scaffolds collapsed
and the trenches collapsed
and their lives collapsed
and their whole bloody worlds

collapsed.

And the teachers came
and the priests came
and the politicians came
and these, the weavers of their destinies,
these seekers-out of brawn,
and not of brain
explained
that it was the will of God,
that it was the way of the world,
then spilled a few self-cleansing tears
and left
the sons
to the mothers that bore them —
and buried them
in cold Slievemore.

Nicola Geddes

comes from a long line of musicians, and belongs to the precariat. Born in Glasgow, she came of age under Thatcher's iron reign and was involved in political activism and NVDA since her early teens. Having studied both Environmental Art in the Glasgow School of Art and Classical Cello Performance at the London College of Music, she has been now been based in County Galway for the past twenty-five years. Nicola works as a cellist and tutor, being an advocate for state-funded arts education, with access for all. To date her writing has been published in *Crannog, the Galway Review, Crossways* and *Skylight 47*, as well being featured on *Poethead*. In 2017, Nicola's poems received a Special Commendation from the Patrick Kavanagh Award, and Highly Commended in 2018 The Over the Edge New Writer of the Year. In May 2019, she won the New Irish Writing poetry competition, with four of her poems published in t*he Irish Times*.

To the Only Agnostic in the Jesuit School

Tell the teacher
you are not sitting
and there is no fence
You stand, bare-footed
on an island of wonder
while all around you
Christians and Atheists alike
sail strong currents
the well-charted waters
of the seas of certainty

Stand tall

my open-hearted revolutionary
Your island has many treasures
and there is no fence

Mary Melvin Geoghegan

was born into a large family. First generation from rural Roscommon—that transition was not always easy, but she came to appreciate the experience of living in a city and having a father who worked in Co. Dublin. Summers were spent helping out on the farm pulling ragwort, feeding calves etc. The freedom of escaping urban life expanded her imagination and at the same time, the cycle of life and death was ever present. She has published five collections of poetry; her most recent *As Moon and Mother Collide* published with Salmon Poetry (2018). She is currently working on a new collection, to be published with Salmon in 2022. She is a member of the Writers in Schools Scheme with Poetry Ireland and has edited several anthologies of children's poetry.

And When Velazquez Stops Painting

his cuticles are stained
in the colour of the jug.
He finds he's hungry, very hungry
he drinks from the jug
lifting it straight out from the composition.
And it's dark beyond the thick-walled windows
of the Palace in Madrid —
All this while the sun has been travelling
over the mountains without him
in another world, from the one he's made.
Which is, nonetheless the same one world
made from stuff.

Anita Gracey

is the seventh child in her family, born into 'the Troubles' in West Belfast. Proud of her working-class background, she has been employed as a checkout operator in a busy supermarket, and as a mentor for those who were, like herself, disabled. She has also worked freelance as a Disability Equality Trainer. Growing up she had dismissed poetry as a middle-class 'highbrow' occupation and not even contemplated it. Upon retiring on medical grounds, she attended a creative writing class and felt a new mode of expression had opened. Since 2017 Anita has been published in in reputable journals and anthologies such as *Poetry Ireland Review, Washing Windows—Irish Women Write Poetry* (Ed. Eavan Boland), *Poetry NI, The Honest Ulsterman, The Poets' Republic, The Blue Nib, The Bangor Literary Journal, CAP Anthology* and Waterways Story-making Festival. She was shortlisted for Hennessy New Irish Writing in 2019.

A Social Worker, a Home-Help and a GP walk into a Service User's life

During the home visit
the client presents herself as capable but has fatigue
she wants a home-help to clean
but there is no budget for cleaners
I'm a social worker not a miracle worker!
I'll get her a cook.
She became argumentative saying
it will take away her skills
getting her a cook would disable her more.
It's beyond my control
I'm here to facilitate.

The travel time don't talk to me — beam me up Sadie!
I'm not paid for this!
Madam the-day put them organic carrots on her shopping list
they're awful expensive so I got her normal carrots,
thinking of her purse
oh did she give me grief!
Said I'd taken another decision away from her
It's beyond my control
I'm phoning in sick the-morra.

She says she feels institutionalised in her own home
eating food which isn't her choice
at times of day which suit home-helps' workload.
Institutional living is people in hospitals or care homes
she doesn't comprehend she's actually very lucky
patients who acquire impairments have a loss of control
this has manifested in her non-compliance
and occasional aggression.
It's beyond my control
I'll prescribe a short course of Temazepam.
That'll do the trick.

Rachael Hegarty

was born the seventh child of a seventh child in Dublin, and reared in the working-class neighbourhood of Finglas. Widely published and broadcast, her debut collection, *Flight Paths over Finglas*, won the 2018 Shine Strong Award. Her second collection, *May Day 1974*, was launched on 17 May to commemorate the Dublin and Monaghan bombings. Her kids say she is a doctor with dyslexia and uses the F word way too much: Finglas, feminism and feckin' poetry.

The Witch Sniffer

The welfare man's a sleveen of a witch sniffer. I must smell
right if I've any chance of getting through the inquisition
for a School Clothing, Footwear and Book Allowance.
You're not going up to that place smelling of petunia oils
and looking like Janis Joplin off out to the gig at Woodstock.
Ma smears lemon rind and juice on me wrists and sprinkles
drops of vanilla essence all over me second-best dress and jacket.
The witch sniffer has a grá for girls who do little but bake and skivvy.
Ma removes me bangles, beads, bauble earrings and granny's brooch.
The heart of the Claddagh ring stares up at me in shock.
She whips off the PLO scarf, zips me jacket, all the way, to the neck
and coils up me tailing-long red hair under a grey woollen hat.
Ma flattens it down, fits the cap snug. She bites at the fat of her lip:
don't look him in the eye, don't let that witch sniffer come near you.

Fried Bread

Hunger's no game. But her robbin' mulvathers me noggin. Thrills me to bits.
She palms sweets from Cronin's shop and pinches apples outta Whelan's
        garden.

One day she swipes her own Da's fried bread. Out from under the grill,
it's scalding hot. Rasher fat still sizzles on the crust. I watch her toss
the slice from hand to hand to cool it down.
She tears into it like a mangy dog at the black bags on bin day.

I don't bagsie her ends. I never eat fried bread.

Mrs. Murphy

The odd time there's a sighting of Mrs. M, head down,
scrubbing out their front porch with a hard bristle brush.
Crimson knuckled, elbow grease, arms reach, going ninety.
A bucket of rinse water. She starts off again. Back into it.

You wonder about the invisible dirt plaguing her doorstep.
One Saturday you see her washing windows. Spy her pale
pink basin of sudsy water and twists of scrunched newspapers
from a hideout behind their garden wall. She says nothing.

Her eyes swollen purple, a gashed brow. Her hands shake.
You leg it, race the street shadows to your front gate,
clutch cold wrought iron in your fists. Wish you could ice
her black eye, Dettol and plaster that gash. Mrs. M needs

to see the state of your gaff: its manky porch and pawed windows.
She should have a quiet word with your Ma and her sisters.

Kevin Higgins

was born in London of Irish parents, grew up in Galway and lived in London again during his twenties. He has lived back in Galway City for the past twenty-five years. He has worked variously as a petrol pump attendant, an accounts clerk, a deliverer of flyers for a North London mini-cab company, and Education Officer at Galway Centre for the Unemployed. He was also for many years an activist and was Chair of Enfield Against The Poll Tax in London the early 1990s. Since 2003 he has made his living as a creative writing tutor and poetry workshop facilitator.

The Restoration

Election results tumble in,
like pinstriped clumps of hairy bacon
being lowered via giant mechanical arm
into a fizzing Jacuzzi
to be congratulated by the media
who have long since discarded their G-strings.

Things as they used to be
have been pasted back together,
or almost, like a vase broken during an argument
or a marriage in which both parties
have agreed to pretend.

Right thinking people will have restored to them
the right to their old wrongs
and for the first time be permitted by law
to order children's teeth on Amazon,
to do with as they wish in the privacy
of their vastly worthwhile lives:

for example
fashion them into impromptu dentures
for their Julian Assange effigies,
or offer as mints to those who got unlucky
and now mess up the pavement
by living on it.

Hoodied Bridget
after Bertolt Brecht & Kurt Weill

You've seen me doing my hours emptying clean
the ashtrays of third hand taxis cabs
and scrubbing hard with bleach their tainted back seats
before they're offered up again
to the god of whatever the market fetches
in a town the government has privately agreed
is to be discontinued, and wondered
what's with her smirk?

You've seen me doing my hours
in the two Euro shop and considered
offering me twenty quid
for a quick ride around the back
of the disused funeral parlour
next door. For you've no idea
what I am.

If you'd any sense
you'd wake screaming
every night in fear of me.
By the time you do
I'll be standing over you
and you'll still be wondering
what's with her smirk?

For there's a crowd coming behind me
carrying a flag you won't believe
you're seeing again
until you do.

You'll go red in the face like an old fool
about to choke to death during sex, and tell me
I'll have fries with that.
For you've no clue who I am.
You'll fumble for your wallet
and toss me a fifty Euro tip, and wonder,
one last time, what's with her
insufferable smirk?

For by then the ship
you thought would never come in
will have quietly docked
flying a flag you'll remember
from the history books.
Its contraband cargo
that will give us the metal to own
everything you think rightfully yours
being silently unloaded by others like me
made what they are
by years looking at the likes of you
poured into your waistcoat, believing in
the divine right of your money.

My pals will be here presently —knock knock—
with their methods of persuasion and
the flag they rescued from the dustbin
in which you tried to bury it.

First question they'll pop
when they see you tied up here
will be *toss him in the skip right now,*
or lock him in the attic for later?

Knock knock knock

A Brief History of Those Who Made Their Point Politely and Then Went Home

On this day of tear-gas in Seoul
and windows broken at *Dickins & Jones*,
I can't help wondering why a history
of those, who made their point politely
and then went home, has never been written.

Those who, in the heat of the moment,
never dislodged a policeman's helmet,
never blocked the traffic or held the country to ransom.
Someone should ask them: "Was it all worth it?"

All those proud men and women, who never
had the National Guard sent in against them;
who left everything exactly as they found it,
without adding as much as a scratch to the paintwork;
who no-one bothered asking: "Are you or have you ever been?",
because we all knew damn well they never ever were.

Rita Ann Higgins

was born in Galway in 1955 and reared in a working-class household in Ballybrit, on the east side of the city. She left full-time education at the age of fourteen where she subsequently worked in many of the factories in the in the Mervue Industrial estate. Rita Ann Higgins has articulated the conditions of the working class, women and society's marginalised since her first poem, 'Dog is Dog is Dog'. Considered a powerful voice for and of the oppressed, Higgins began writing poems in her early twenties, and has since gone on to publish over twelve collections of poetry, essays, prose and a number of dramas. She was a columnist for *The Sunday Independent* and is a member of Aosdána. 'No One Mentioned the Roofer' first published in *Ireland is Changing Mother* (Bloodaxe 2011), 'Grandchildren' first published in *Throw in the Vowels* (Bloodaxe 2005) 'Our Killer City' first published in *City Tribune 2017*, later in book of the same title (Salmon 2018).

No One Mentioned the Roofer
(*for Pat Mackey*)

We met the Minister,
we gave him buns, we admired his suit.
The band played, we all clapped.

No one mentioned the roofer;
whose overtime was cut
whose under time was cut
whose fringe was cut
whose shoelaces were cut
whose job was lost.

We searched for his job
but it had disappeared.
One of us should have said
to the Minister,

Hey Minister, we like your suit
have a bun, where are our jobs?
But there was no point;
he was here on a bun-eating session
not a job-finding session.

His hands were tied.
His tongue a marshmallow.

Grandchildren

It's not just feasible at the moment
one daughter tells me.
What with Seamus still robbing banks
and ramming garda vans when he gets emotional on a fish-free Friday
in February.

Maybe the other daughter could deliver.
She thinks not, not at the moment anyway
while Thomas still has a few tattoos to get,
to cover any remaining signs that might link him with the rest of us.

Just now a B52 bomber flies over
on its way from Shannon
to make a gulf in some nation's genealogy.

The shadow it places on all our notions is crystal clear and for a split
of a second helping
it juxtaposes the pecking order.
Now bank robbers and tattooers

have as much or as little standing
as popes and princes
and grandchildren become another lonely utterance impossible to
pronounce.

Our Killer City

Galway's bid to win Capital of Culture
is all twenty twenty give the horse plenty.
We're in with a great chance,
until they hear about
the legionnaire's disease outbreak
in the fire station,
where our life savers need saving.

The birds are tweeting
about the arrival of the jury this July .
The word is out they'll rule on the bid.
Best to keep them councillors out of sight,
with the malarkey they go on with, in city hall.
Govern, govern my arse.
They wouldn't govern a sly fart on a runway.
We'll end up crowned the capital of fools.
Accusations of nepotism, potassium,
a host of other isms, chisms, chasms and schisms.
I sent you that letter by mistake
said the CEO, buckling under pressure.
You are not actually co-opted
onto those committees,
FYI, you are co-workered off.

My ogyny, your ogyny, misogyny.
We laugh about it at bus stops.
We say, aren't some of our
elected representatives a laughing stock.
We'll never get Capital of Culture
if they look through that window.

Some people live their lives
so they can die on a trolley
in Galway's A&E.
Just wait and wait and wait
and you'll die waiting.
Eighteen million on a new block
and not a new bed in sight or on site.

The car park police in the hospital grounds
are a culture shock unto themselves.
Don't die on a trolley in the bidding city
the forbidding city,
before you have paid your parking
or we will kill your next of kin
with the weight of their parking ticket.
Culture Capital or no Culture capital.

The swans in the canals all know,
we underpay our nurses
we underpay our teachers
we overpay our consultants
and we don't know why.
This is fair-play city, or unfair-play city
if you are a woman working for years in NUIG
and hoping for a promotion.
Hashtag-go-Micheline-go.
They'll sue the blog off ya,
but won't they look silly,
don't they look silly.

This is pity city, shitty city.
Sewage in your nostrils city.
This is Galway
city of expert panels.
City of slickers and slackers
who name-call Travellers knackers.

If you want the odour of outrage
ask the students at GMIT
who have to re-sit exams.
Allegations of cheating.
Oh no not this again.
They are coming in July to rule on the bid.
We'll hide that bit of news about the GMIT
and the gender discrimination in NUIG
in the parlour that never gets used.
To that we'll throw the new block,
the bed-less block at University Hospital Galway.

This is Galway slicker and slacker.
Have your home burgled
by your favourite nephew,
while you are at his other aunt's funeral.
He didn't know it was her house
and he didn't know taking her jewellery
without her permission was stealing.

This is Galway the bidding City
the forbidding city.
Where the woman in court apologised
to her man for putting him through this.
The judge asked her, did he apologise to you
when he was sticking that screwdriver
in your forehead?
No but he wasn't feeling himself that day
your honour.
Someone in City Hall, not a councillor this time,
is yowling about the Capital of Culture bid.
If the bid book isn't ready on time
says the yowler,
I'll send you all to the fire station
or The Picture Palace.
She is pepping and prepping and side-stepping.
Her side-kick got side kicked. No impact.
Complaining is the devil's work.
Stick in a few more theatres
that we don't have, stick in a gallery or two.
How will they know if it's true?
How will they know if it's not true?

This is Galway, city of tools.
A man brings a cleaver into hospital with him.
The judge coming down with a migraine,
reached into her bag-a-yokes.
What got into you, she said,
pleading with the plaintiff?
I heard the chops were tough your honour,
nothing more, nothing less.
But you were seen chasing the back

of a poor man's head, with a cleaver.
It wasn't me your honour, and he wasn't poor.

What about local artists?
Someone dared to ask,
not the yowler from city hall
or her side-kicked side-kick.
To hell with local artists
what do they bring the city?
Nothing but scruffy dogs
and ripped jeans,
hippies with hobbies the lot of them.
As for the buskers, wanting to fit in
with the odour of outrage.
Move them on, hide them in GMIT,
or The Picture Palace.
Don't mention local artists at all.
Let it be like they don't exist.
Raise the rents is the best way
to keep the ripped jeans gang out,
like its always been.
Artists me arse.
This is Galway, the bidding city
the forbidding city.
City of thieves or is it scribes or is it tribes?
The jury are coming this July,
the word is out they'll rule on the bid,
for Capital of Culture
twenty twenty
give the horse plenty.
We have a great little city here,
a pity little city, a shitty little city.

Jennifer Horgan

is a teacher and has worked for the last 13 years with kids in East London, Abu Dhabi and Cork City. She is interested in the stories of the people behind the headlines. She is deeply concerned with the treatment of women, both in Ireland and abroad. The abortion referendum meant a great deal to her. A couple of her poems explore Ireland of the past, with the hope that we can better navigate our future. She is a mother of three young children.

Tuam Babies

Damp and green
the garden frames our warming.
Same shape and grain
as when you'd drive me out to school
and back again.

Along the bank
you mark the knot-still-forming
Dried-out earth
long-term dearth of flowering.
With thanks to God you understand
sieving mud through ageing hands
years of trying patchy growth.
The strangeness of a single rose.

It's a good thing you've come home

Your weed so furiously fused
that we must both remove
pull and drag it to the sack,
until halved and heaving you approve
and I relax.
File in sands, a saving grace
You
Your woollen jumper, muddied hands.

This no burial ground
to cover violence
Simple truth in unmarked silence.

Older clots still bleed anew;
I crawl inside the good of you.
Small hollow mouths
round out pain
To dig, dig, dig them out

Home again.

villanelle for us
(*Housing Crisis Ireland 2019*)

on the 216, counting lights in traffic
rain thick against the window
listening to *Joe* above the static.

library's closed, so 'no panic'
when the driver slows
on the 216, counting lights in traffic.

when I'm Big, I'll be a Medic
fix your cough that grows
listening to *Joe* above the static.

you say, I'm such a 'Tonic'
where are you, when I'm in school, Rose?
on the 216, counting lights in traffic?

we have to pay to be in public
a man in a carpark died, froze,
listening to *Joe* above the static.

they said it was 'Only Tragic'
but it was more for those
on the 216, counting lights in traffic,
listening to *Joe* above us, static.

Paul Jeffcutt

lives in the Brontë Country of Northern Ireland. His father worked in a factory, his mother worked in an office. Paul went to technical school but became the first member of his extended family to go to University. He began writing in his spare time. His debut collection, *Latch*, was published by Lagan Press (2010). Recently his poems have appeared in *The Honest Ulsterman, The Interpreter's House, Magma, Orbis, Oxford Poetry, Poetry Ireland Review, Poetry Salzburg Review* and *Vallum*. He has won 28 awards for poetry in national and international competitions in Ireland, the UK and the USA. 'Dear Sir or Madam' was first published in *The Poets' Republic 6* (2018).

Dear Sir or Madam

Please forgive this intrusion
I folded your new tablecloth
stiff and cool
and I had to write.
Be most assured I do not ask for favour
nor indeed for money
though heaven knows our times are hard as the frost
that grasped my throat as I trod to work today
the sun's low beams striking the mist
above the bleach green.
Gentle sir or madam
I do not wish to trouble your comfort at breakfast
whether partridge
smoked herring
or a brace of bantam's eggs
but I implore you
hear me out.

I am a lapper
and have been these dozen years
since father passed
a position I gained as a lass
that detains me for most of God's hours
six days of the week
and puts bread into hungry mouths.
I will not presume upon your knowing

the complexity of this trade
suffice it to say that mine are the last
of many hands which turn humble flax
into the fine cloth that spreads before you.
I have heard it said that linen
fashioned by our hands
graces the finest tables
from Chittagong to Valparaiso.
Truly does the sun ever set upon our works?

Kind sir or madam
I must not burden your patience
any further
I am an honest Godfearing woman
and I ask you this
please raise a prayer
for the labouring poor of the parish.

Your faithful servant in the lapping room.

Fred Johnston

comes from a family (North) of trade unionists and one of them a budding Communist, (he ran for the old Stormont as 'Labour' and holidayed every year on the Black Sea). His father suffered for his shop-steward activity. Fred's family on his mother's side (South) didn't do much of anything and nothing at all political. He was 'blacked' in Dublin for unionising the public relations industry in the early Seventies—as his father warned him that he would be.

Testament

God brought him forth out of Egypt: he hath as it were
The strength of an unicorn......

My father said that, since I was still workless,
He'd get me into the shipyard. Harland & Wolff,
Queen's Island, duncher caps and bicycle clips.
My grandfather was secretary to the East Belfast
Boilermakers' Union — sons after sons in their tribes.

Well and good, all this; it helped if you belonged
To a Lodge.
Clan writ ran the length of the rails and the height
Of a gantry. I squinted at the grids and girders

Saw in them an infinite cartoglyph, read the
Signs and codes, the black mass of men herding
Over the bridge out of their Egypt, a treacle of black bees:
All of it an intimate speech of sorts, whispers through the iron;
A job for life, rivet and scalding steel, tea from a tin.

All well and good; a word in the open ear, keys
To a Jerusalem of water and iron. Not for me.
Not mentioned again.
Not spoken of, building arks like Noah, tossing them
On the waters like bread: no Moses to whack the tide in two.

Never Again

We might begin by asking what we'd do
In a similar situation. How we'd be, or who
And what might be the reaction
       When doors fall in and the screaming starts
       And those young men, tutored in the arts
       Of terror, once again visit us.

We ought to ask such awkward things
We ought to wake to our tidy days on wings
And have a moral stake, if you like
       {The clichés here fly like bullets, like shells,
       It's almost impossible otherwise to tell
       A yarn so deplorable, yet so banal.}

Yet I think that to survive, for others to survive
We must quit the moribund battle-cry, the lie
The long-blunt instrument of justification —
       Language must be remade to be even half-true
       It is the least this generation can try to do
       Swear truth to ourselves forever, like a vow of love.

My Father at Niagara

How he came to be there was a navigation upwards into light
Both of us framed with our backs to the lens in Kodak black-and-white
How he came to be there with his son in such roaring liquid light:

We're leaning on an iron rail peering into a madness of water
Fragile as pufflings on a ripped cliff, sure of falling, the candour
Of tumult so blazingly raw and blinding and made, absurdly, of water

Under that awful sound and rage he may have heard an iron voice
Or glimpsed the oracle signaling of the rightness of his choice
To leave the shipyard city with rust in its throat and sectarian voice

Come out to a new land, dig in unfamiliar soil, lay in new ground
So that, with luck, his mother-coddled son would reshape the sound
In time of so much water plunged under bridges, so much gone
        underground.

John D. Kelly

was a brought up on a working-class housing estate in Belfast and was aged nine when 'the Troubles' erupted in 1968. For many Catholic parents, education was one way for them to potentially help their children get beyond the culture of sectarianism, employment/ social/ housing discrimination, and the insidious control of organized religion endured by their generation for decades. John qualified as an architect in the mid-eighties, survived that recession, and has worked, precariously since then, in many areas of the profession including social/ public housing. Following the most recent recession, he studied psychotherapy (a lifelong interest alongside poetry) and now practices in two 'low-cost' and 'no-cost' counselling centres in Dundalk and Belfast. He has his poetry commended and published in many literary competitions, magazines and anthologies. Currently, he lives in Co. Fermanagh and is working on a debut collection.

Teenage Kicks

You have to love your monsters as well as your angels.
That's what my big sister Mary used to tell me, years
ago, before she saw red, and the light, and left the convent.

In 1979, the long hot summer was over and I was going
back—hell-bent—to the hellhole that was my school.

Geldof was still cool then, and I was walking up the Falls
Road, and it was a Monday; but it was The Undertones
then this that was ringing in my ears: *There are
procedures to be followed; there must be 'accountability* . . .

I was remembering the strap line of Brother Punctilious.
It stopped me in my track: . . . *kicks right through
the night* . . . I was already late, but this was the procedure
that morning: *Assume the position! Spread your legs wide!*

Arms were soon high, palms open, body leaning, facing
into the red brick wall; off balance, waiting . . . waiting.

I made *Teenage Kicks* keep ringing in my head
even though they had already smashed my new Walkman
under big, black, shiny boots.

Give only your name, even if they beat you with the butts
of rifles, or kick your feet wider apart, to stress you more.

My brother had primed me. He was in the same position
in 1971, but be couldn't hold his tongue and it lashed out.

He spent the next three years interned in a cell, living
with *his* monsters. His girlfriend, Angela, waited, waited . . .

and waited. She ached wet for him, through the dark years.
Our broken mother's tears dried up when she died, in 1973.

Our bereaved father still goes to mass, but alone now,
even though Mary also left *her* cell, and her other 'sisters'

in 1974; no longer willing to accept the habit, the order
the procedure – the having to 'keep mum' to cover
the exposition of the barefaced 'men': those uncountable
monsters; monsters that, still to this day, live mirrored
in the innocent faces of grown-up children;
that other, sick unaccountable army of black and white
uniformed pretenders — 'fathers' who whispered:
Spread your legs wide—for God's sake—my 'daughter'!

Andrew King

is a teacher. He has worked with girls from disadvantaged backgrounds in Dublin city centre and has seen the difficulties faced by young girls in sidelined communities, wherein both economics, race, and gender often act as seemingly insurmountable barriers. Andrew writes both prose and poetry and has had work published in both Irish and English. Some publications that Andrew has previously featured in are: *The Brain of Forgetting, Icarus, Revival, The Cathach, YEWF, The Attic,* and *Tuathal.* Andrew has won and received runners-up prizes in the following competitions: The Dromineer Literary Festival Short Story Prize, The Drogheda Arts Festival, The Francis Ledwidge Poetry Prize, The Listowel Festival Poetry Prize.

Echo

On the cold steps of the criminal court,
her father clung to her mother,
while their lawyer described their little girl
as a young woman like any other —
she loved music and dancing
and she loved to sing.

She'd sing like a nymph on Mount Cithaeron,
mirroring the muses' moves,
dreaming she was an icon —
and she'd look the part
with her shimmering hair
and her makeup done
the way she had learned on Youtube.

This one time, she thought she loved a boy,
a fair-haired, well-built Narcissus,
but he had loved his own looks more,
so the love that she felt was fictitious.
When it was over, she'd scroll through his photos —
though it hurt and she'd cry,
she still did it.

Alone and lost, the word *femicide*
was a knot of slim vowels with no meaning.

She knew no meant no, so she didn't know how
her no could be seen as misleading.
But Pan saw the Oread's
seemly singing and dancing
and thought no was just playful teasing.
He was a God, after all,
the ruler of shepherds and wilderness,
from rustic Arcadia,
a companion of Nature,
his lovemaking was famous.

CCTV last saw her walking alone —
they put this last still in the paper —
an oblivious gaze through the grey, speckled haze,
with no signs of imminent danger.
But her no burned red in Pan's hot rage,
his pride pricked by indignation,
so he drove men to savage and rip her to shreds
to pay for his emasculation.
Frenzied, the shepherds did as he bade them —
Like wild animals, they tore her apart
and scattered the still singing fragments
of her body across the earth.

Gaia wept at what they had done to her,
and so hid her broken limbs
among valleys and quiet outcrops
and the silence of sleeping mountains.

Those fragments of her life
still scream and call and sing —
a listening-mirror of perfect likeness
for the sounds of all earthly things.
When we laugh, she laughs,
when we shout, she shouts,
when we cry, she cries.
When we speak the names
of the women we've killed,
she speaks them too —
Annie and Eva

and Imelda and JoJo
and Ciara and Fiona
and Deirdre and Emer
and Jasmine and Sophie
and Jastine and Ana.
She says them after us,
one by one,
so that in the Echo
we can hear her again.
And we can hear ourselves.

Anastasia Kiourtzoglou

Originally from Greece. Kiourtzoglou has been working and living in Ireland for the last 12 years. She tries to bring humanities, sciences, and arts together for a better present and a brighter future.

INVOLUNTARY IMMIGRATION
I, Nasrin Mobayen

I	Immobility
N	Numbness
V	Voices
O	Optic ataxia
L	Loghorreic characters
U	Unanimous chaos
N	Nebulous gazes everywhere
T	Trying to fill bags
A	Accelerating a loath departure
R	Renouncing a detrimental present
Y	Yanked from us
I	I, Nasrin Mobayen
M	Migrating to the unknown
M	Modern Amazons in battle
I	Invisible female warriors
G	Girls bleeding profusely
R	Rotten boats
A	Abysmal boarding
T	Tenacious holding
I	Irritation
O	Opaqueness
N	Necrosis

Immobility
Numbness
Voices
Optic ataxia
Loghorreic characters
Unanimous chaos
Nebulous gazes everywhere
Trying to fill bags
Accelerating a loath departure
Renouncing a detrimental present
Yanked from us

I, Nasrin Mobayen
Migrating to the unknown
Modern Amazons in battle
Invisible female warriors
Girls bleeding profusely
Rotten boats
Abysmal boarding
Tenacious holding
Irritation
Opaqueness
Necrosis

Paul Laughlin

lives in Derry. A former Secretary of Derry Trades Union Council he has published three collections, most recently *Conflict Studies, New and Selected Poems* (Lapwing Press). New work currently appears in the *Poets' Republic 7* and the *Glasgow Review of Books*.

Nation, Flag and War

When the state affirms an anniversary
Or sanctions a centenary
It speaks of sacrifice and legacy
Of what they mean for you and me
But who are the banners unfurled for
If the rich stay rich, the poor stay poor
And the old lies still obscure
The truth of every wretched war
What remains of our fine aspirations
Nurtured over the generations
Has every promise been made good
Each pledge in turn again renewed
Or long since ceased to resonate
With the queues at the departure gates
Countless days stand as the anniversary
Of some exercise in futility
That will serve somewhere as a victory
If no one asks what we're cheering for
While the rich stay rich, the poor stay poor
And all the old lies still endure
In nation, flag and war

No Fit State

In this sclerotic state where
Things are seldom looking up
And never moving on
The crowds begin to gather
For the annual parade

The mind-set never changes
The speeches stay the same
Always passing off as culture
Things that cover us in shame

Those that can get out
And live in their own way
Those left behind are in no doubt
That misery moulds their every day

Patients wait on trolleys
For a doctor to arrive
The newly homeless
Sit in doorways amid
The wreckage of their lives

News has yet to reach them
Of all the progress we have made

Michal Lowkain

was born in Poland in 1974 poet, and is a vegan and lefty (a word often used as an insult in contemporary Poland). His parents were the first in their families to go to college. Michal's seven maternal uncles were workers; his mother was always proud of her roots and into anti-authoritarian leftist politics. The family (four children) was poor. Michal attended a dual system second level school, combining the leaving certificate with vocational training in construction. He studied Sociology, worked as a journalist for the biggest newspaper in Poland, but the job was precarious. He is a Dubliner since 2006. For the first six years, he worked as a manual worker in an alarm system company, was then made redundant, and used the payment to study sociology in UCD. After a period of unemployment, he worked as an advice worker for a charity organisation. In 2013, Polish punk publisher Jirafa Roja published his poetry book *rzeczykrwistość* (*bloody reality*—poems with the author's photos and photo-graffs). Ballyfermot is his place on earth now, having previously lived in Dublin 8 (Liberties and Dolphin's Barn). The poems used in this anthology are Lowkain's first to be published in English.

d8 (with fate)

not really a nice post lady
(at least to an immigrant on the dole)
alky shaking every morning
(chain smoking till having his cure)
homeless madman — a picture of marx
(eat the bleeding rich!)
polish neighbour knowing everything about everyone
(kurwa!)
irish neighbour on detox
(oh sweet fecking dreams!)
irish neighbour on hera
(same neighbour)
muslims next door — teetotallers
(surely)
women in their pyjamas on the streets
hordes of men in their tracksuits
young user constantly vacant
(new in the area)
locked pregnant lady
(delivery before long)
adonic shop assistant non-stop chewing a gum

(every body loves him)
blonde redhead looking like my dead friend
(accident when drunk)
old man — like my old man
(don't like my old man)
bartender disrespecting the ones ordering juice
dozens of riotous young mothers with prams
dozens of boisterous bhoys with bottles and pot
drunk female calling her partner a wanker
(he's too drunk to wank anyway)
crowd in penneys che tees
(¡hasta la victoria siempre!)
punks locos winos junkies
rubbish on the streets
closed shops spaces pubs
fallen people and animals
and you out of the blue
grew the red roses
into it

(!
  palaces
       the
          on
            war)*

* This slogan alludes to the revolutionary German writer Georg Büchner's 1834 call "Friede den Hütten! Krieg den Palästen!" ("Peace to the shacks! War on the palaces!").

race to the bottom

my manager in the alarm system company said
if i were black i'd have everything for free
free house free food free healthcare free fecking all
probably even sex for free and i'm not talking about me bleeding mot
but i'm white innit?
so i need to pay for everything

weeeewooooweeeewooooweeeewoooo

how do you know it john paul?

fuck off will ya?
read news check facts connect the dots
ask any black on the street if they pay for something
we're working our arses off
literally
we're working as slaves for them
and for travellers
and immigrants of all colours
it's a shitty rainbow man

i'm an immigrant john paul

but you're different you poles have always great work ethics
(yeah means work more for less and keep your head down)

weeeewooooweeeewooooweeeewoooo

male worker: listen bud two black ladies used to work here
they were lazy lazy as fuck
they were doing nothing
i think the boss doesn't want them blacks and others here
only whites he wants

female worker: yeah and there was a nigga once
his food was so smelly he ate outside 'cause we couldn't stand it
smelly fella he was

really the guy ate outside? for how long?
(no sense to discuss n-word
before: don't be a nigga-lover you can't trust them)

male worker: a year or so
but he left i think he didn't like the job
he didn`t like working didn't like working at all i'd say

fuck sake guys you're a bunch of bleeding racists
(i tried to say it as a kind of joke)

weeeewooooweeeewooooweeeewoooo

female worker: i am so wha?
male worker: nah i`m not it's just the facts
manager: this country's dying man europe's dying
we are in deep shite
end of story

hey have you ever heard about direct provision?

they didn't
i tried to tell them about
production of broken people
about locking people up
in shelters
mostly people of colour
feeding them
building mental prison
burning their hope
driving into alienation
depression
madness
the tougher and creasier the system
the less asylum seekers here
degrading
humiliating
inhuman
kids there
kids born into this

impossible but still possible
like always

manager: you see everything for free!

weeeewoooooweeeewoooooweeeeewoooo

after some time the owner sold the company
without saying a word to us
(it was a family business
we all like a family here the boss's daughter informed me
with a smile when i started
maybe it was a joke?)
so all the racist pricks
talked about workers' rights then
one day a new guy came
he was small grey hair grey eyes grey suit
whiteness in its greatness
hi i'm your new boss how are you?

i didn't know
they got us
after all
everything is possible
in this sorry
fucked up world
(like
white workers hating
their comrades
and loving
white bosses)

weeeewoooooweeeewoooooweeeeewoooo

Gearóid MacLochlainn

was born on the Falls Road, Belfast. He has published five collections of poetry in Gaeilge and three books with translations. He says that "growing up during the Troubles in West Belfast meant experiencing myriad ideas of working-class identities and clashing ideologies that fragmented and exploded any broad-based notions of working-class solidarity. After the Civil Rights Movement there appeared no hope of working-class unity in the North. Fortunately my father was a pacifist Marxist and his perspectives helped me get through a very confusing upbringing in politically splintered, fractured, and deeply sectarian, divided working class, that was once Belfast. Today, things are changing for the better and I would define myself optimistically as a utopian-anarchist-socialist, for what it's worth."

Heatwave Eile

Bhí an boladh bréan ag análú
ó leithreas briste síos sa Choirceog Beach
róláidir inniu. Dofhulaingthe.
Bhí mo phoill sróine ag damhsa
le *sewage* an *heatwave* órga
a ghlac seilbh ar an chathair
seachtain ó shin.
Bhog mé go dtí an gairdín ar chúl a' tí
le bheith ag caitheamh.
Bhí an áit folamh go fóill.

Tháinig mé go luath roimh lucht na gcapall
le píosa de *Séamus Ennis — Dialann Taistil 1942-45*, a léamh,
leabhar a fuair mé ó Áine sa Cheathrú Póilí
ar *bargain* praghas ...

Bhí Ennis ag seanchas faoi *Ediphones*,
wax cylinders, tyres a phléasc sna *potholes* ar dhrochbhóithre Charna...
Thosaigh mé a mhachnamh faoi tharr Mac Adam
agus Dunlop ... agus *inner tubes* ...
nuair a tháinig Arutura isteach
agus é ag iarraidh orm line nó dhó a chumadh
fá choinne amhrán nua *hip hop* Gaelach s'aige ...

Bhí sé ag gearán go raibh sé dúthuirseach ag iarraidh bheith liked
ag daoine geala, agus tuirseach de Ghaeilgeoirí Dearga
nár thuig a chuid Gaelachais ar chor ar bith! ...

D'éist muid le píosa den amhrán ar Mac s'aige,
muid frámaithe ag seanfhocail Ghaeilge ar an bhalla in aice linn —
NACH RAIBH FEAR BRAITE RIAMH I DO CHUIBHREANN
GO RAIBH DO DHEOCH LÁN BRÍ IS BEATHA
DIA IDIR SINN AGUS AN URCHÓID agus araile ...

Trasna uainn thar bhalla eile bhí seanséipeal na mban rialta,
brící rua ag crithlonrú, dreoilín agus lon ag ceol
sna driseacha a d'fhás thar an bhalla.
Bhí seanstaighre iarainn meirgeach
ar thaobh na láimhe deise
chuig doras an halla damhsa ar bharr a' tí
a bhí druidte le fada an lá.

Go tobann thuirling scamall ón Chnoc Dhubh.
Bhí beirt fháinleog mhí-stiúrtha agus faoileán ag peannaireacht
is ag líníocht leo sa spéir liath ...
Stop an ceol.
Thosaigh Arutura ag seanchas liom faoi mhuintir s'aige —
Ní raibh siad róthugtha don rud scríofa,
don pheann ná don phár,
rud a thug an cine geal leo
nuair a tháinig siad leis na bíoblaí.

— Tá *totems* níos tábhachtaí ná teanga, arsa sé,
Ba *hippopotamus* mo mháthair mhór.
Níl cead ag éinne lámh a leagan orthu
gan bheannacht s'aicise.

Rinne sé adharca beaga ar a éadan lena mhéara
— Agus cad é mar a déarfá i mBéarla ... bíonn
siad amuigh ar an mhachaire?
— *Gazelle* ...?
— Sea! Is *gazelle* mé féin. Clann *Antelope*!

Agus cén fáth nach gcreidfinn é?

Nach seanchapall mé féin? a shíl mé ...
Níl ann ach seal ár gcuarta.

Bhí *staff* ón King Kebab ag cúldoras na cistine
ag snórtáil línte sneachta roimh am oibre.

Las Turo dúidín agus tháinig cumha air.

— An rud nach dtuigeann daoine geala
faoi Mugabwe, arsa sé, ná ...

Go tobann,
bhris *hum drum* leictreachais
agus raiméis innealra ó na *generators* is *coolers*
a bhí ar a dé deiridh le fada,
isteach ar an chomhrá.
Clagarnach, cniogaide cnagaide ...
Thart orainn bhí crónán cáblaí,
cluncanna agus clancanna seaninnealra,
cuisneoirí ar crith, ag croitheadh a gcnámh,
ag cogaíocht le cloinceanna is clanganna eile,
Nuts, bolts, blades, belts, shudders, shakes
miotal ag sú isteach aer te na maidine,
meaisíní, ingearáin sna ballaí.
Ní raibh dul as.
Maraíodh ár nglór ag an challán chrua.

Ansin, stop sé de gheit,
Sos cogaidh. Tost ...
Puth gaoithe sa bhrothall.
Scuabadh an scamall ar shiúl.
Scaipeadh na liatha.
Phléasc an ghrian anuas orainn arís
ó bharr an tSléibhe Dhuibh,
gathanna gréine ag spréacharnach
ar smidiríní de ghloiní briste ón oíche rua roimhe,
soilsí órga ag rollagú inár súile
leis an toit liath gorm dubh airgead,
muid ar snámh le scáthanna *hippopotami* faoi uisce,
ag rith trí mhachairí le *antelope* adharcacha,

greadadh na gcrúb, cosa in airde,
fainleoga mí-stiúrtha ag peannaireacht arís
trí ghormacha na spéirlíne,
Ar feadh bomaitín bhí muid beirt
chomh Gaelach leis an ghrian ...

Chaith muid ceann eile is thit muid siar
isteach sa *heatwave*.
Bhí an saol ar a sáimhín só
i gcroílár na gCeathrún Gaeltachta
ciorraithe.

Another Heatwave

The stench breathing
from the broke-down-bog
in the Beehive bar
was too strong today
my nostrils were jigging
and tickled by sewage
from the golden heatwave
that possessed the city
for a week now

I moved out back to the garden to smoke
The place was still empty
I came early
before the horse punters
to read a bit of Seamus Ennis' Travel Diary, 1942-46
a bargain I picked up from Áine
in An Ceathrú Póilí bookshop

Ennis was updating me on Ediphones,
wax cylinders, bicycle tyres that exploded
in potholes on bad back-roads of Carna...
I was pondering tarmacadam, Dunlop...the inner tube...
when Arutura called in

He wanted me to help him with a lyric
on his new Gaelic hip hop tune...
He was giving out, saying he was tired
Of trying to be liked by white people
and tired of Gaeilgeoirí Dearg le Fearg
who didn't get his Gael Gorm side at all...

We listened to the tune on his Mac
We were framed by Irish proverbs
on the wall beside us--
MAY A SPY NEVER SIT AT YOUR TABLE
MAY YOUR DRINK BE FULL OF LIFE
GOD BETWIXT US AND ALL EVIL...etc.

Across the way behind the far wall
was the old convent chapel
red clay bricks shimmering,
a wren and blackbird trilling
in the hedge that drooped over the wall.

The twisted rusted iron staircase
on the right led to the dance hall
at the top of the house
that was shut down
years ago...

Suddenly a cloud descended
across Black Mountain
There were two swallows and a gull
sketching and scribbling
in the grey sky...

The music stopped
Arutura began to tell me about his people
How they weren't won over by pen and paper
or bibles from the whites

—*Totems* are more important than tongues, he said
My grandmother was hippopotamus.
No one could lay a finger on one

without her blessing

He made two horns on his forehead
with his fingers
—And how do you call it in English...
They roam on the plains?
—*Gazelle*...?
—Yes! I am a gazelle. Antelope!
And why wouldn't I believe him, I thought
Sure I'm a knackered horse myself
We are only here for a spell...

The staff from King Kebab
were at the back door of the kitchen
snorting snow
on a smoke-break

Arutura lit up
And became distant
—The thing white people don't understand
about Mugabe, he said, is...

Suddenly the humdrum
of electricity, the rattle of machinery
from the old-pub generator and coolers
that were on their last legs
broke up the chat

our voices were buried
by moaning cables
clunk clanks of wire bone cages
warring with clang-clinks
nuts bolts fanbelts shuddering
spinning blades
shivering refrigerators
souls of rusted hardware
lined along the walls
under the awnings
in the corners...
There was no get away.

As suddenly as it started
it stopped.
Silent,
a puff of wind in the swelter,
a cloud brushed away,
greys dispersed
and the sun exploded again
on top of bottle-green Black mountain
beams flickering on smithereens
of broken glass from the night before
golds rolling in our eyes
of silver blue smoke
we swim submerged
shadows of hippopotami
we run across plains
antelope hooves
pounding again
unruly swallows
sketching and scribbling
the blues on the skyline

for a moment we are both
as Gaelic as the sun.

We lit another smoke
then collapsed back
into the heatwave

life was hunky dory
for a spell
in the heart
of the cut-up
Gaeltacht Quarter

Tomás Mac Síomóin

Born Dublin 1938. His mother was from a Dublin working-class area, the Liberties; his father's stock were Roscommon hill farmers and active IRA militants in the Irish independence struggle, 1918-21. The first member of his family to have third level education, he worked in factories in England in the 1950s to pay his university fees. Early membership in the IRA influenced his formation. His translation into Irish of *The Communist Manifesto* was published in 1975 by the Communist Party of Ireland, of which he was a member. His interest in the Irish language stemmed from periods spent living in the Gaeltacht. A Cornell University, NY., doctoral graduate, he was a biology researcher and lecturer in the USA and Ireland. He edited the Irish-language publications, *Comhar* (a literary cum current affairs monthly) and *Anois*, a weekly newspaper. He published collections of poems, short stories as well as novels in Irish (some translated into English). He has also published non-fiction, such as *The Broken Harp: Identity and Language in Modern Ireland*, which examines the enduring effects of colonial brutality on the Irish. He has written in, and translated from, Spanish. Has resided in Catalonia since 1998. Poems in this selection first published in *21 dán/poemes/poemas* (Coiscéim, 2010), collected poems in Irish, Catalan and Spanish.

Anaxagoracht

In anam dubh an tsneachta
tá rún gach samhraidh
breacaithe
glascheadal fras
gach earraigh
is fómhar
an chaoinspioraid leacaithe
rún
nár scaoileadh fós
dá bháine

Anaxagorism

In the black heart of snow
all summer secrets
are inscribed
the generous rains
of distant Springs
frail Autumn's
russet secrets
all unsuspected
by your whiteness

Iceara

Ar bhain moill bheag duit, a Icarais
is tú id' sheasamh ar imeall na haille
sular léimis thar bhruach,
meáin an tsaoil mhóir ag faire
ar sciatháin an ghaiscigh ag bualadh
go ndeachaigh as amharc?

Ar phéac síol amhrais id' chroí
sular chraithis do sciathán céarach
sular thugais cúl le scáth is ceo
agus aghaidh ar léire na gréine?

Nó an bhfacais i gcroí d'aislinge
an tsúil fhuar dhall ag oscailt
snáth searbh do scaoilteoige
ag béithe na cinniúna á fhíochan?

Ach léimis ina dhiaidh sin;
roinn liom, a ghaiscigh, an rún
a shnaidhmfeadh dhá leath mo dhíchill
le sciathán dána céarach!

Icarus

Did you pause a moment, Icarus
as you stood on that cliff-edge
before you took off
a worldwide audience watching your show,
the beat of a hero's wings
as they passed from sight?

Did doubt sprout in your heart
before you shook your waxen wings
taking your leave of shadow and mist
for the clarity of sunlight

Or did you see in the heart of your dream
the gaze of that cold blind eye
as the bitter thread of your shroud
is woven by fate's indifferent handmaids

But you leaped aloft for all that
share with me, o hero,
the secret that welds halves of riven hearts
with the beat of waxen wings

Beethoven sa gCeoláras Náisiúnta

Ruabhéic bharbartha faoin gceol
i measc na gcarbhat is na gculaith
fir thatúáilte ag rince
thart timpeall tine chnáimhe
a bhronnadh teas is solas
feadh oíche fhada na coille

tá fulacht fia á fhoilsiú anseo
is cnámha crinnte toirc
tua garbhchloiche
saighead na rinne cnáimh
is cnámhóga na tine úd
atá múchta anseo le fada

ach mothaím ruabhéic bharbartha
ag gleáradh faoi screamh na bhfocal
fear tatúáilte ag rince
faoi charbhat is chulaith

Beethoven in the National Concert Hall

Barbarian howl beneath the music
Among the ties and suits
Tattooed folk dance
Around the very fire
That gave us warmth and light
In the long night of the forest

A stone roasting pit is here
wild boar bones
a rough stone axe bone arrowheads
cinders of a fire that died
before our history dawned

Still that wild barbaric howl is heard
Beneath its crust of sound
Tattooed folk are dancing still
Shackled by collars and collars

Seán Maguire

was born in Belfast. He left school at 16 and worked in manual jobs before studying for 'O' and 'A' Levels. Seán obtained third level qualifications including a BA Hons in Humanities with English Literature. Seán's writing journey began with writing song lyrics for his friends' punk band. In 1998 his poetry collection *Harvest Soul* was published by Sessyu Press. In 2017, a collection of poetry called, *For Those Left Behind* was published. These poems reflected on what Seán described as the *human debris* of political conflict in the north of Ireland. Seán's poetry has been published by *The Cringe* (Australia), *Poetry NI, Panning for Poems, A New Ulster* magazine, *Pangolin Review, Poetry in Motion* annual anthology, *Nine Muses Poetry* and *Unity*. Seán has worked for over thirty years in the community sector and been active in trade union activities through NIPSA and Newry Trades Council. 'Pawn Shop Deals' was first published in *A New Ulster* literary arts magazine August 2018.

The Other Side of Tomorrow

Flashbacks of burnt-crusted skin,
dripped in warm showers of melted
candles. Wounded voices, screamed
out for mentors, during panic attacks
in crowded shopping centres.

Away from homely comforts, anxiety
enforces its grip on frail minds, in wedding
confetti storms. Blind steps were taken
to the past, to bomb-damaged buildings
where the trauma was cast.

Weak to the bone, the future
choked in scorching forests
of yesterday's pleas, to rescue
survivors before the other side of tomorrow.

Teenage Tricks

In the mid-seventies, life spun in a parallel world,
my best friends were aliens, long before Star Wars,
E.T. or American Dad. Kids were entrusted to run
down schools, obsessed with rules and regulations,
adding to the frustrations of being misunderstood.

Music, and books kept me intact. I made Faustian
pacts with David Bowie, and Tom Sawyer.
When boredom struck, we split into groups to play
a game of 'Brits and Rioters'. It was like the real thing.
Bricks and Bottles rained down on those without riot
shields (dustbin lids), waves of pretend snatch squads
used sticks instead of batons. The chases were great
fun and kept us on our toes, there was no obesity then.

The highlight of Saturday afternoon was 'Big Daddy'
and 'Giant Haystacks' sporting straight faces as they wrestled
with reality. We swam in lakes and pools, did country walks,
stole our parents' beer, smoked cigarettes, but our biggest
fear was talking to girls, at the Tuesday night disco.

Pawn Shop Deals

We arrived for the game,
a bunch of scrawny school
boys, shorts inches below
our knees.
There were no changing rooms.
We togged out, behind the old
chestnut trees.
The school pride was at stake.
Minutes, after the whistle blew,
teeming rain turned the pitch
into a man-made lake.

My boots were way too small,
I could barely walk, never
mind run or kick a ball.
No protests were made,
they were the pawn shop's
best deals,
with a communion dress
and pink coloured pram,
sporting baby blue
wheels.

Marc McCann

works in a mental health environment and every day encounters people who are living on the outskirts of our society, the shadows almost. These are damaged and broken individuals in many ways and he believes the focus of his poems is to shed some light on their struggles and how they are often misrepresented in society.

Medicated

Cannabis induced psychosis
GPs give out Prozac doses
Cans of cider help me focus
When I watch T.V.

High dependency alcohol unit
Morphine tablets get me through it
With diazepam I can do it
And lots of cigarettes

Post traumatic stress disorder
Take cocaine or something harder
I'm a sleeping tablet martyr
I don't get much sleep

Methadone withdrawal symptoms
Red bull helps the nervous system
LSD for my autism
Painkillers ease the pain

Kiera McGarry

was born in Larne, Co. Antrim. Much of her childhood was spent playing outside her grandmother's house in Ballystrudder estate in Islandmagee. She also helped on the family farm at the weekends, owned by her late grandfather, which she continues to farm with her aunt Deborah. She went on to graduate from Queen's University Belfast with a PGCE in English, and currently works as a teacher. Her work, widely published, has featured in books such as *New Poets of the North of Ireland* and several literary journals such as *The Open Ear, Abridged, the Oghan Stone*, and *Poetry Ireland Review*. She has just completed a poetry project funded by the Arts Council of Northern Ireland.

Clipping

Behind the clatter of mechanical teeth
the clipper tosses you your first fleece of the day,

loosened by the quickening blades.
You begin the ritual of gathering the wool,

feeling sheep-skin grease sting the cuts
on your hands, folding it in on itself

until the springy coils bunched tight
as butter bricks. The very fibres of you

know the routine set before them,
to pick and tear the dung clods

and maggot sweat-nests apart
from clean and golden stretches

of unsoiled pelage, to hunch over
the clipper's table like a knuckle

for hours. In the days after
the clip is done, you find white hairs

on your clothes, the sprung wool strands
uncoiling like a sprig of cloud —

you feel the ache of exhausted muscles
that still twitch to roll and fold again,

hands still smooth from the oils
of the fleeces, the work that softened all edges.

A Memory of our Grandfather's Hands

We saw them again in the grandson
he would never know. When he was born

he was unlike any newborn thing
I had held or known —

grasping, wriggling, gloriously pink.
Black eyes, gorgeous as acorns.

His hands, roiled and unfolding,
clasping his ruddied cheeks, huge

like spades. I wanted to fill those hands
with chicks overflowing, soften them

with the moil of a shorn sheep's fleece.
In time they learned to angle toy tractors

down imaginary lanes, haul grass
in miniature trailers made from lego blocks

into cardboard silos. Every night,
the tractors will haul silage

in his dreams: we are there together
hand in hand in his restless kingdom

of grass, shadows of hot green flecks
whirling from the tyres of the machines.

We are watching with heads tilted back
like two drinking ducklings.

Elizabeth McGeown

was raised in a Housing Executive house in working-class Belfast with both parents on benefits. Today, she has a limited income as she works part-time for health reasons. She is the 2019 winner of the Cúirt International Festival of Literature Spoken Word Platform, two-time All-Ulster Poetry Slam Champion and a finalist in the 2016, '17 and '18 All-Ireland Slams. She was chosen by judges from Dublin: UNESCO City Of Literature to take part in the Lingo Festival Slam 2015, placing third in the same competition in 2016. Featured performances include Body & Soul, Loud Poets Fantastical Game Show Spectacular, Lingo, Sunflowerfest, Sonnet Youth, C.S. Lewis Festival and the Edinburgh Fringe. Her first e-pamphlet, 'twas, was e-published by Pen Points Press in December 2018.

Divided Land

In Northern Ireland there are things you don't talk about
In the 1960s people learned the hard way to stop
Silenced in the '70s with a bitta jail time if you didn't comply
Unlike the '80s when they wouldn't stop talking
So much they were reduced to mime, a crime to be heard, absurdly
      dubbed
The '90s when talking turned to singing, they pretended to hold hands
      to teach the world to sing
Somewhere in the middle of all this, I appeared.

Maybe I absorbed it in the womb, absorbed the whispers and the bin lid
rattles like I absorbed my Mother's nutrients like they absorbed their
own nutrients from their fat and muscle and bone marrow until nothing
was left. It took him 66 days to absorb himself and I think, in the womb,
I heard it. I'm made of it. McGeowns only last 42 days before their family
take them off strike for health reasons, you can't die as it'll make you sick,
as only a McGeown can manage to fuck up dying

I am your red right hand. I am this divided land.

I didn't realise 'Zombie' by The Cranberries was about Northern Ireland
as everyone has their tanks and their bombs and their bombs and their
guns, don't they?
Memory: A fire was just a fire and I laughed because I didn't know
why there was a guy on the top as that was 5th November, remember
remember I read it in books? My Mum hushes me, saying she'll explain

later, not wanting the neighbours to know I don't know it's the pope
because I was sheltered from all this, living in interdenominational bliss.
Never heard the sash, don't know it when people ask me to sing as I live
in a bubble, in a bubble, in-

I am your red right hand. I am this divided land.

Came up the Lagan, up the Lagan in a bubble, in a protective bubble
in my protected protestant school while McGeowns were dropping like
flies all around me, all warm and safe save for the glowing neon surname
attached to my forehead. No-one ever spoke of it. Francis Felix became
Frank, Anglicised, Franklicised and I never wondered why he didn't
come with us to see the bands.

A Catholic taxi driver shot dead. This is what the news is for, to tell
you who's been shot. I didn't even understand half the words but can
still hear them now with a kind of muscle memory: Secretary of State
Tom King, Patrick Mayhew, Tom King, Patrick Mayhew, paramilitary
shooting, kneecapped, found dead, found dead, shot dead. This is what
the news is for, to tell you who is dead.

We didn't take the soup he said but people keep force feeding me.
McGeown. McGowan? McGeown. McKeown? McGeown. McGewan?
McGeown. McGeown. McGeown!

I am your red right hand. I am this divided land.

Word association! Burnt out car, car bomb, petrol bomb, bomb scare,
        bomb scare,
bomb scare, Castlecourt (normality), bomb damage, fire damage sale.
I never wondered why so many places were on fire.
Some places were afire more often than not, which led to cheap school
        uniforms.

Memory: in the library, made some friends and I can pinpoint the exact
        moment
"Are you a Protestant or a Catholic?" and time stops.
More words from the news, the news to tell you who is dead. Protestant
and Catholic and I resolve to find out what they mean when I go home.
Should I have been listening all along?

I am your red right hand. I am this divided land.

I take pieces of evidence out and examine them.
What exactly are people doing to each other's kneecaps?
Why do the Orangemen carry swords?
Why are they so unhappy? What if their sword slips?
A secret fear, every year I edge away from the spikes.
A grey spot on a happy day. Is it a happy day?

A Catholic taxi driver shot dead. This is what the news is for, to tell you
who's been shot.
I didn't even understand half the words but can still hear them now with
a kind of muscle memory: Secretary of State Tom King, Patrick Mayhew,
Tom King, Patrick Mayhew, paramilitary shooting, kneecapped, found
dead, found dead, shot dead. This is what the news is for, to tell you who
is dead.

I am your red right hand. I am this divided land.

Derided man
Black and tan
Home rule plan
Balaclava football fan
Also ran
Weapons ban
Kickin' the can
I'll tell me Ma
I am this divided land.

Poverty is pink

Words that don't logically go together but came to mind just before sleep
  and wouldn't leave
So I stored them, as words before sleep are often a precious gift
Poverty is pink

Like the school dinner tickets
No-one told me until I was 8 years old that I could eat every day for
free and I wore my pink ticket like a badge of honour, proudly going up
to the teacher each day to claim it before the others who had to queue
shamefully and pay.
Gorging myself on the milkshakes,
The dinner lady jugs of cool, wet strawberry bubbles,
The cake with pink icing submerged in pink custard,
I wolfed it down, all the sickly pink.
The ham and jam and spam.
Could carve shapes in the spam if I didn't look too closely at the brown
gelatinous edges, the pitted surfaces filled with white fatty deposits.
Chew, chew, chew.
It was all free.
Poverty is pink.

Felt-tipped pens are precious things.
I had a set with orange, brown, two greens, turquoise. The finest shade
of pink you ever saw and would only use it once a year, to colour the
tiniest morsels. The fingernails of a doll, a drawing of Christmas lights.
Lids on immediately, no oxygen here. Back in the packet into a tin
box which went on a shelf. Everything was shelved and protected. We
knew the value of a good pink. Tins of Roses and Quality Street were
recycled for years, filled with precious objects found on the ground:
a shiny pebble; a child's lost badge; a car number plate written on the
card inside a chocolate wrapper when playing Columbo. All memories
memorised and logged and rose-tinted. Those rose-tinted glasses that
make poverty look pink.

Those Global Hypercolor t-shirts that were everywhere, dripping their
globules of heat-activated colour all over Primark shelves and everyone
who was anyone glowed gently in purple orange glory. My parents shied
away from the price so I fell in love with a waistcoat in a bargain bin in

the worst of charity shops. 25p and I sat proudly over dinner, mashed potato warmth and pink protection worn for years until it became rags. I was the pink one, I shone rosy when I wore it. My sister was blue. She suffered blue for years, because she was older and missed an economic upswing which brought charity shops on every corner. Couldn't wear whatever she liked, the eye searing colours that I picked for myself in the bomb damage sales, so bright I would never be hit by a car, they joked. Allowed to buy one thing from the pound shop and chose the thickest pink polish, letting it dry petrol-scented on my nails and picked it off in clumps.

We made our own perfume in the working class. Snuck into gardens and we quiet as meeces ripped those gardens to pieces, choosing the petals of
Rose, Hydrangea, Rhododendron,
Rose, Hydrangea, Rhododendron
in a green thumbed frenzy, mincing and shredding in bottles of water, shaking the mixture and gently scenting the water. The scent never lasted overnight. Nothing ever lasted overnight. Except the memories. The sweet-scented, rose-tinged memories.

Scott McKendry

is an electrician and a student at Queen's University, Belfast. He's read at events on both sides of the Atlantic and published work in the anthologies *The future always makes me so thirsty: New Poets from the North of Ireland* (2016) and *Happy Browsing: An Anthology in Praise of Bookfinders* (2018) as well as the following journals: *Poetry Ireland Review, Magma, The Tangerine, Public Illumination Magazine, The Manchester Review, Cyphers, The North* and *Virginia Quarterly Review*. McKendry has a pamphlet forthcoming in June 2019 with the Lifeboat Press and is working on a full collection called *Hammer & Environs*. 'Duck, Duck, Goose' was first published in the *Virginia Quarterly Review* in early 2019.

Duck, Duck, Goose

You can go down for a jouk, I want to say, a gander
at the greylags on the green
that's not so much a field as a grassy space
where the flats once stood.

They come at the end of November,
fleeing the Icelandic freeze; swapping the aurora borealis
for murals in memory of Stevie McKeag
and Bucky McCullough;

and those for Cromwell, Cúchulainn, Luther
and Iron Maiden's Eddie the Head
dressed up as The Trooper, moonlighting for the UFF.
Widespread throughout Eurasia, the greylags

of the steppes often winter
on Inner Mongolian paddy fields, where they eat rice.
But on this estate, they make do
with Tayto crumbs and cones of dropped pokes.

When a local finally stuffed one for Christmas dinner,
a scrawl went up on the courthouse wall:

LET IT BE KNOWN
AS WITH TOURISTS
GOOSES TO BE LEFT TO THEIR OWN DEVICES

Helen of Foreman Street

To this day, wherever there's an ottoman,
my da sees his ma on it in her nightie

cradling a forty-ouncer of Vat 19
the way she'd held him. The favourite child

of a dozen, he'd chase the loanshark from the door
— down Killarney, across Conlon,

round the Henhouse and by the swings —
often only in his socks and trunks.

My da's ma drunk called him a dirty rat
when the headmaster sent her a letter:

Your lad, who hasn't been to class in weeks,
ran through the playground in the altogether ...

Jesus he has some funny stories,
like the one where she stabs him.

He lives; but today he sulks between rooms
like a guilt-tripped ghost. And having lost

the taste for the sauce altogether
after a spate of pratfalls this year past,

he now can't sit apeace when we're on it,
so we send him up to his cart.

Because he can't stomach velveteen cushions
or the voice of that man on the BBC,

he has his breakfast, dinner and tea
standing at the counter in the scullery.

Paul McNamara

is a writer, performer and college student from Limerick. He also works as a college tutor, bartender, writer and front of house at a theatre to pay the bills. He is a two-time All-Ireland Spoken Word Slam Runner-up (2015, 2016), a former Munster Slam Champion (2016) and Yeats' Tower Slam Champion (2016). He works has been featured on TV3 and RTÉ Radio and festivals such as Indiependence and published widely. He has also written and performed two poetry plays: *Hello, My Name is Single* (Limerick Fringe Spirit of Fringe 2019) and *Quarter Life Crises* (Galway Fringe Spoken Word Award 2018).

Nations or Notions?

A full Irish, bacon and cabbage, a cup of tea and a ham sandwich
Irishness in 24 hours, with maybe a digestive thrown in for good
        measure
And let's say a pint of Guinness or four if it's a Saturday

Watch the news at 9, the Simpsons at 6 and if you happen to be sick
Judge Judy at midday or Jeremy Kyle if it's a particularly bad day
And if you do happen to be sick, flat 7up and Vicks should do the trick

Watch GAA but secretly love football even though you call the players
        babies
Compared to the rugby, love rugby players, no matter what, unless they
        become politicians
Hate all politicians the current crowd are always worse than the last and
        the last crowd were
A crowd of fecks who fecked the place

Hate all politicians except the ones who went to your great granda's
wake, and your gran's and gran uncle's and anyone you know who ever
died, like a politician serial killer would go far because funerals equals
votes, or they can just get you planning permission on the sly boy

Hate the feckin' Gardai,
Who fine you for driving just barely over the limit no matter how much
you plead, when last month they never caught the fella who did stabbing
in the city, but sure my uncle says they are only trained to catch the
middle class in Templemore

But most Irish people are kind to everyone rich or poor, unless they're
        English,
But mostly we're friendly and merry and drunk and Religious, but these
        days only on Easter and Christmas,
And politically unexpectedly actually relatively democratically progressive

And we love Katie Taylor and Conor McGregor and the O'Donovan Brothers
Love the young offenders and the rubber bandits and of course
Migeldy Higgins, who gets a pass for being a politician, because he's
Great craic, and has no real power anyway
And whether you're in business the arts or well anything, apply to be
        president
Everybody's doing it

Say yes to equality and yes to choice
And nope to the pope and hope to be
Killed before being associated with the Donald.
Proud of your county but only when they win,
Support local sports at least when they are played by men
Be proud of the flag, no wait that's an American thing
Be proud of the government no feck that hate every politician
Support local arts though mainly only when they're foreign
But feck it be grand sure what would you be doin' payin' for a drawin'
By the fella down the road, what a load of bollocks, you already paid for
A licence for the TV, that's enough funding for the Arts scene (they tell me)
But look it's not all bad, the weather seems to be getting better during the
        summers
Which is good for the farmers, at least for about two days until the country
most famous for rain runs out of water yet again, well feck

Noel Monahan

was born in Granard, Co. Longford and grew up on a farm there. He worked as a teacher of History and English for thirty-six years. He is now a full-time writer of poetry and drama. He has won numerous awards for his poetry and writing. His awards include: the SeaCat National Poetry Award, organised by Poetry Ireland, the RTE P.J. O'Connor Award for drama, the ASTI Achievements Award, the Hiberno-English Poetry Award and the Irish Writers' Union Poetry Award. His poetry was a prescribed text for Leaving Certificate English, 2011 and 2012. To date, he has published eight collections of poetry. 'Hymn For The Tuam Babies' was published in *Chalk Dust* (Salmon Poetry 2018).

Hymn for the Tuam Babies

Look at them
Prayers on their lips, carrying dead babies
To unmarked graves.

And the nuns said:
And the priests said:
And the politicians said:
And in truth we all said:
Let this cup pass from me
Because there's no cup, no bushel,
No tank large enough to stash away our guilt,
No goat or Cardboard Box Man
To haul our sins away.

How long more must we continue
The never-ending quarrel with ourselves?
How long more must we put up with
A jealous and vengeful church?
How many more women, and children suffered
And found themselves put away?
Tiny corpses scattered like dung
In septic tanks
No stone to mark their names.

But the missing stone has seven eyes
And the lamp-stand of seven lamps

Throws shadows on the walls
Of women carried off at midnight
To unholy convents and homes
Under the so-called watchful eyes
Of Church and State and its people.

Let us all go down now
Into the pits of darkness
And let us cry from the depths of the night
And raise the baby bones to the light.

Unhappy Prayer

When crows were white
And Gorgon's blood revived the dead,
Silenus, the pot-bellied one
Mounted an ass, headed for the city

To meet Midas,
(Urban chairman of the golden handshakes)
And there at the market square,
He defended
His anti-natal thoughts:
>   *The best thing for man*
>   *Is not to be born*
>   *And if alive*
>   *To die as soon as possible.*

Last Outpost to the Gods

Mainland.
How are you!
We are just another island,
                                   Cut off.

It's one Big Theatre of Cruelty Here.
Dia Mór agus dia beag
Who's holding the gun to God's head?
Everything is becoming too hot
The lid won't stay on the pot
We need to save ourselves from ourselves
City streets full of open manholes.
No corncrakes, no curlews, few hares ...
All walking in someone else's shoes
Shouting for legal rights for robots.

All the rainy islands in the West
Spoke Irish and starved.
But the boot's on the other foot now:
No priest, no doctor, no Post Office,
No bar to drink or talk in
It's all down to the behaviour of words now.
As the priest once said on Inishmore:
Send us boats or send us coffins.

Pete Mullineaux

is from a working-class background; he grew up in Bristol UK but has lived in Galway since 1991. He has worked with numerous arts/community/campaign groups throughout Ireland, using poetry and drama to explore social and political issues. He has published four collections of poetry, most recently *How to Bake a Planet* (Salmon 2016) and critics have compared him with John Clare, Roger McGough, John Cooper-Clarke and Pete Seeger. Pete has also had three plays produced by RTE Radio and was invited onto Arena to discuss his writing. As part of his work with Afri (Action from Ireland) he's published an educational resource: *Just a Second—Exploring Global Issues through Drama and Theatre*.

Tonight's the Night

I took Dad to see Neil Young; he wore his suit (Dad, that is —
Neil Young wore a tie-dye shirt.)

1975 (I think) Bristol Colston Hall: crazy Neil with Crazy Horse.
And crazy me for bringing Dad

but he'd taken me to Cheddar Caves, Castle Coombe, and over
on the ferry to South Wales —

(again, Dad, not Neil Young, who wasn't taking me anywhere, yet.)
So I wanted to show him something,

even though his taste in music began and ended with Bing Crosby;
(*definitely* Dad, not Neil Young

whose influences would be well, more blues, roots country
and rock and roll.)

And he was cross: (Neil, this time; my dad was surprisingly
mellow, if somewhat conspicuous.)

They started with a brand new song called *Tonight's the Night*
which the audience heckled

wanting more familiar tunes like *Southern Man, Helpless*
and *Cowgirl in the Sand.*

But Neil was having none of it — he gave us all a lecture:
how this was about someone

real close to him, a roadie who had died from drugs —
'Bruce Berry was a working man...'

and sang it again, only more aggressive; which pissed
the audience off even more.

I was hoping Dad was OK, not feeling out of place
but he seemed to be taking it all in

even nodding his silver head through the deranged
twenty minute guitar solos.

Eventually there was a compromise: the band
won us over by doing all the old hits

but then, for an encore did *Tonight's the Night* again.
I'll never forget it,

afterwards, he bought me a takeaway, (Dad, not Neil Young)
don't know what Neil and the band got up to

maybe they went back to the hotel
and talked about an old guy in the third from back row

who had smiled all through the concert,
and wondered what he was taking.

Whatever, I enjoyed myself too —
felt Dad and Neil Young

had got on well together.
'Bruce Berry was a working man...'

Child Soldiers

'Military Manoeuvres' — Thomas Moynan 1856-1906
National Gallery of Ireland

They wear the uniform of poverty —
bare feet and rags, a motley parade
of innocents. Led by their general
wielding a sweeping brush, one
carries a wooden sword like an
upturned cross, another blows
into the spout of a metal can —
his comrade whacks a bucket;
this mesmerised urchin, staring
out of the canvas has no weapon —
a conscientious objector?
A genuine soldier looks on, somewhat
befuddled, neat tunic and brass buttons,
hat tipped forward as if slipping from its moorings.
A girl with a basket watches, unsure.
A well to do couple stroll by on the other side,
the man carries a tennis racket.

Familiar neutral grey tones of an Irish town
but everywhere, patches of red —
the soldier's jacket, the crimson shawls;
beneath one rust-red roof an unidentifiable
blaze glimpsed through a narrow window;
three scarlet ribbons trickle down
from a paper helmet; the rosy cheeks of
the boys and girls.

Free Range

The Chinese low-paid workers
who roasted in the fire
that speedily engulfed their factory,
who were cooped-up
along with the chickens they handled,
who like their feathered companions
had little choice in the matter,
who threw themselves
at the peeling paint, padlocked door,
scratched at windowless walls,
tried to leap above the flames —
who were not free range,
who were —

David Murphy

Much of Murphy's written work reflects the precarious lives of those rooted at the foot of the neoliberal economic pyramid. His poetry has been widely published in magazines and anthologies in Ireland and abroad, including *The Poetry Bus, Stony Thursday Book, Revival, The Burning Bush, Irish Literary Review, Cyphers, The Ogham Stone, The Stinging Fly, Poetry Ireland Review* and *The Shop*. Also a short story writer and novelist, his latest book was published by Dublin's Liffey Press.

Narrowing Path

An envelope falls from her hands.
She heaves a billowing sigh at
that mounting trove of manilla.
No light, no heat — utilities unpaid
in her thin-walled fifth-floor apartment
built for negative equity.

On an empty road cranes stand
silent as graveyard crosses,
immobile as jobless husbands,
quiet as homeless children.
At their feet a discard
of construction helmets like

clusters of yellow-white limpets
around legs of crumbling piers.
A study in hushed dereliction:
boarded-up buildings,
office block tombstones,
streets grey with mist.

City of shadow and opportunity.
Hoodies prowl alleyways
on racers stolen from public places.
Wheels slick on wet tarmac,
swapping scrapyard promises
for another set of broken vows.

Connivances, nods and winks,
the dole queue or the aeroplane.
Speculators eye fifth-floor apartments;
moneyed men slither and slide,
wheels shed lives like water splashed
from puddles — rims buckle, frames rust.

Spokes take the strain; nothing changes at the hub.
Pain is measured in neoliberal doses,
not in colosseums as Romans did,
but in amphitheatres of the market
ruled by Petrochemical Gods, I.T.,
Big Pharma and Media.

Nero's fiddle pines for lost empires
consumed with greed and the well-to-do.
Embrace enterprise, tax the poor,
indemnify the rich. Speculation,
Janus of all Profit, knows no bounds.
In the Pantheon of care-less culture
all doors lead to Bread and Circuses,
a sophistry of excess; our narrowing path.

Stepping on Stones

As I waited on the corner
a poor boy asked me for some change.
I rummaged in my pockets,
told him I had nothing loose
except a screw or two like ones
that hold my mask in place,
the theatrical mask that slips
when corners of my mouth turn down.

I left the poor boy in his cage,
avoided shifty men carotid with rage.
Exhaust fumes belched against me.
Hard-nosed women garrotted each other
with sharp-edged shopping bags.
I hurdled the feet of beggars
and resolved to leave this city
to its chains of ghostly bankers.

I wandered far from fields Elysian
to a place undesired. Harbour lights beckoned.
Dreadlocked men in a tumble-down shack
sold me a one-way to a place where
there is no psychotoxic news
to wake me in the morning, no current affairs
to tuck me in at night. Radio phone-ins
are unplugged, talk shows silenced.

Bonuses remain unpaid except in the
case of hospital cleaners, road sweepers
and other worthy recipients;
a just and equitable place
where Plato's advice is taken
and the differential in pay
between highest and lowest
is no more than a factor of five.

Frank Murphy

is a satirist of the class realities of Ireland. Winner of the Jonathan Swift Creative Writing Award/Poetry 2009. Shortlisted and placed in many others including Listowel (Humorous Essay) 2017. Also Swords and the Jonathan Swift 2017. Others going back include the Oliver Goldsmith, Francis Ledwidge, Domineer, Boyle. Published in many places.

All Washed Up

Getting closer now
That rumble in the distance,
Winds picking up
Delinquent
Signs.

Peeling
Off street corners
Easy deals
Drunk in the sun
Crimping,
Down notices to quit.

Shooting
Up back lanes
Window-boxed high-rise
Lifts out
Abandoned cars

Flights of fancy
Flapping on the clothes line
Liberation movements
Threatening rain.

A Knight's Tale

With chaptered verse
To course his veins
He quarried out his own demesne
Set off to find the Holy Grail
Then crept along the paper trails
And naked in his stirrup cups
He'd fleece you from the bottom up
And tilt upon the dotted lines
He lived in interesting times
And tiring of such daring deeds
Drew sustenance in other creeds
Such prospects as would tilt your hat
Noblesse oblige no less than that
Allowed such little license pleased
Himself to charge
Professional fees.

The Market Dictate

They tell you it's great
Down in subsection four
On the set-aside farms
Where they lock up the poor.

Who'd forgotten to file in
Before it's too late
Now they're serving the needs
Of the Market Dictate!

As the credit runs out
On your permit to walk
Outside on the pavements
Nobody talks.

The neon reminders
Read out from the wall
That the Bicycle License
Collector will call.

And if you've done nothing
There's nothing to hide
So trade in your name
For the numbers inside,

Yeah! Trade in your name
For the numbers inside
Put an x on the spot
Where democracy died.

Kenneth Nolan

Born 1977, raised in council estates: Blanchardstown then Tallaght. Founder of 'The Merg Sessions': a poetry/prose showcase event with the aim of providing a creative platform for writers from non-privileged backgrounds. Published in *The Irish Times, Scum-Gentry Online, A New Ulster, Flare, Live Encounters* etc. Shortlisted for the Jonathan Swift Poetry Award, and the Bailieborough Poetry Award Winner: CDVEC Award for Poetry. Inspired to write via the works of the great 19th century Irish poet James Clarence Mangan. He received a basic education as a child, though has since enjoyed the benefits of adult education and is now a mature student at Maynooth University studying Philosophy and Ancient Classics. He passionately believes in the importance of freedom of expression and independent thinking.

Night Bus to Jarfalla

It almost makes it worthwhile;
the bus journey, in the dead of night.
It collects us from Farsta Centrum,
at 1am. François and I
angry, cold, chronically tired.
I hope that the six hours graft ahead will be bearable.
It used to be good craic with the boys
on the shift in Jarfalla.

François has a handy number these days,
at the scanning bay.
He is less miserable.
I am destined for the Vasteras Truck
my permanent post;
a forty-foot Container, to be emptied in three hours.
The lightest package weighing forty kilos.

I yearn for 5am, then things will get a little easier,
myself and three other lads
assigned to unload the air-cans.
Until then it's three hours of the hardest graft available in Jarfalla.
Alone in the V-Truck.

The lads jokingly compare it to:
being sent to 'the hole'
in prison terminology.
And it's always with a despairing amusement
that I view the duty sheet for the week ahead.

On the concourse wall every Monday morning
I see my name, under the title:
Vasteras — 2am to 5am.
The eleventh, twelfth, thirteenth,
consecutive week.

Before the new boss Paul from England took over,
you only ever worked one week at a time on the V-Truck.
Now it seems I am stuck in it.
The little breaks I have when the conveyor-belt jams
I fantasize about dismantling his face
with the spanner I use to get the belt going again.
Notions of diabolical violence, previously alien to me.

Noted by all: the unfairness
of the same person, stationed on the V-Truck constantly.
"Why don't you say something to H.R.?"
a colleague enquires;
I'm a month away from completing my trial period.

The little victory comes at five minutes to five.
Shaking the hand of Jasper the cab driver,
filled with hate, I throw Paul a cavernous glare;
I am sure he can read my mind every time:
Fuck you, you English cunt
I made it!

The other side of the coin.
When the deadline is not met,
nor looking likely
come quarter to five.
He will let me fail, rather than allow
lads who are idle
help me.

"What happened this morning Irish?
It's not rocket-science!"
I don't know Paul.
Maybe if I could have a little help now and then...
and stop calling me Irish, my name is Kenneth.

Those days are long gone
and I don't miss them much.
I don't miss the Vasteras Truck.
Though, in the dead of night
sometimes I lie awake
and think of
the night bus:

the majestic ten minutes travelling from Soder,
over the Vasterbron bridge;
water beneath, courage in heart,
I am McAlpine's Fusilier
'No money if I stop for rain'.

Onto the main island
the night bus tiptoes past Gamla Stan.
I look on, eyes exalted
the wonderful city of Stockholm a-beckoning!
Out through Odenplan
past the bright blue houses of Solna.

I am Che Guevara.
Then we come to a road sign.
It reads:
'Jarfalla 2 kilometres ahead'.

Plague Pit*

Lounging at the feet of olive-green hills
When I walk her streets, misery pervades
Poisoner of my soul, haunt of my ills
Empty promises, hatred marinades
Round hole with Square; ignoble crawling peg
Filtering memories devouring dreams
False public image, social powder keg
Grief scorched faces, Lego-block housing schemes
Ugly part of town revealed in my speech
Cathedral for the poor; forgotten class
Engulfs like a syndrome, Plague Pit beseech
Bitter voice calling out; snake in the grass!
Life's distillation, every chromosome
A stray mongrel dog, she follows me home

[* The place name 'Tallaght' is said to derive from the Irish *'tamh-leacht'* meaning 'plague-pit'].

Mícheál Ó hAodha

is a poet who writes in Irish. He grew up in Galway, the eldest of 11 children, and worked in the North of England for many years. His translation of Galway-born writer, Dónall Mac Amhlaigh's novel *Deoraithe* entitled *Exiles*, chronicling the working-class experience of Irish migrants to England during the 1950s will be published by Parthian, UK, in April, 2020. His chapter 'Socialist Literature in Britain: The Traces of the Irish Working-Class' appeared in the volume *Marxist Perspectives on Irish Society* (Mícheál O'Flynn et al. —Newcastle, UK: 2014) and his essay 'Limerick and the World—The Limerick Soviet, and the Legacy of 1919' appeared in the anthology *Let Us Rise: 1919-2019: An Anthology Commemorating the Limerick Soviet 1919* edited by Dominic Taylor and John Liddy —Limerick: Limerick Writers' Centre Publishing (2019). His most recent book is: *Leabhar na nAistear 2*—Coiscéim: Baile Átha Cliath (2019), from which all three Irish language poems below were taken, translated into English by their author.

Ag Fanacht ar an Leoraí Oibre
(*Na Duganna, Learpholl*)

ag seasamh sa sneachta, ag seasamh i dtost
an toitín deireanach á shú síos go bun
smaointe grá is díoltais, smaointe díoltais is mó

Waiting for the Work Lorry
(*The Docks, Liverpool, England*)

standing in silence, standing in the snow
last cigarette smoked to the butt
thoughts of love and revenge, mostly of revenge

148

Ó sea, agus rinne mé dearmad a rá leat...
(*Do*: Paula, Striapach (Kensington, Learpholl))

Ó sea, agus rinne mé dearmad a rá leat...
An oíche dhorcha úd is mé ag siúl abhaile,
Rinne mé dán de d'aoibh gháire thnáite

Oh yeah, and I forgot to tell you ...
(*For*: Paula the Prozzie — Kensington, Liverpool)

Oh yeah, and I forgot to tell you...
that one dark night when I was walking home,
I made your tired smile into a poem

Nithe a chuireann tú i gcuimhne dom a mhac...
(*Litir Mham*)

grian na maidine a shuíonn ar do shean-geata adhmaid
éin bheaga sa chrann úll
gan aon ní caillte go deo
do sholas is ruidín de mo sholas-sa ann...

Things that remind me of you, son
(*Mam's Letter*)

the morning sun that sits on your old wooden gate
small birds in the apple tree

nothing lost forever
your light with a bit of my light in it...

Alan O' Brien

was born in 1977. He was raised in the Finglas/Ballymun area of Dublin, and is a bricklayer by trade. In opposition to *emigration culture*, he returned to education in 2011 and received a BA in English-History at UCD, 2015. He also received the Dublin City Lord Mayor's Certificate in Oral History 2016; was shortlisted for the Maeve Binchy Travel Award 2015; was winner of the P.J. O'Connor Award 2016, and finalist for the Lingo Spoken Word festival 2016. He has been published in *Rabble* magazine, *Travellers' Voice* and *Liberty* newspaper. He co-wrote, directed, and took a part in a play entitled *From the Backbone Out* that was performed in Liberty Hall, Dublin 2016 and 2017. An academic paper by him on Irish Literature is forthcoming in literary journal, *Fulcrum: an annual of poetry and aesthetics* 2019 Cambridge, Massachusetts.

An Margadh Gombeen 2016

The Gombeen Market 2016

American-wake, for yet another of our daughters!
I join a congregation in observance of the traditional style,
And we wish that on her life's road she will not falter;
"Slán leat a deirfúir!!..and goodbye...goodbye".
Bopping-on-down through Dublin's 'cultural quarter',
I twist, skip and avoid pickled-humans-fried
Be the Irish culture of drugging-up lambs for a slaughter,
And the green-neon shamrock-sign beckons, "Come buy... diddleyie...
        Come buy".
Then, for the solace of the north-side by the Iron-duke's crossing,
And anxious for the solitude of an afterhours emptied Henry Street,
Yet a dormitory for the homeless is there for my greeting
While a resonance of words from one hundred years repeat:
Cherishing all the children of the nation equally!
Cherishing *all*... the children...of the nation...equally?

Labour Estranged 2010

We stood in that line, a queue,
For we're required to sign. Here, there were new folk
And *used* folk, all through, 'tis true.
We shuffled and rippled; nobody spoke
Except some children that shout in play with the echo
That reverberates the walls of that unemployment hall...hall...hall
Some of us lurched and rocked to and fro
Chins on chests, guttural snorts and all
The sad eyes, lost eyes, indifferent eyes,
Searching neck-napes like search lights.
An argument erupts; a little baby cries;
The hatch shut abrupt, slammed down tight.
In my mind a fertile thought occurred like a desert taking rain,
That the cost of a loss can be the currency of a change.

Ireland, are you drunk on 800 years?

Ireland, my Ireland, are you drunk on 800 years?
"No son", says she, "the past hundred could drive a country
To drink, *don't you know?* Sure the liquid form of fears is tears.
 Those that hold all gold, passed it on to their own fold, only.
Imperial-pain all about; although it's supposed to be gone.
So, they separated the arrogant-rich from humble-poor
And 'twill be that way everafter, for all. Denied my true poet's body, home;
Sure always to violate my childer they come. Hid & helped behind shut door!
And those that spoke for my childer were put in toil,
To be experimented on. No, not drunk on promises, or years,
Like my childer with Tiger-promise; a macrocosm of the Boyles
In Juno. No I'm not drunk. But, I am prepared for renewal, you hear?!"

'If thus o'er one life's blotted page some neutral soul should bend,
They'll read today-as yesterday-a story without end.'

[Final couplet from Dora Siegerson Shorter's poem *The Story Without End* circa 1917]

Jessamine O Connor

grew up renting and moving from place to place in mostly very middle-class areas of Dublin. An only child of a working mother, she was highly aware that low-paid workers often worked harder and longer than the professional parents she grew up around, with no security, and in her case no home to show for it. A single parent herself for many years, she has lived in the rural west of Ireland since 1999 and is currently studying for a BA in Writing and Literature in Sligo IT. Her poems are widely published, including in *The Stinging Fly, Abridged, Agenda, Poetry NZ, New Irish Writing, The North, Shot Glass Journal* and *Skylight47*. She has five chapbooks of these poems, and her first full collection is coming out with Salmon Poetry in early 2020. She is a winner of the Poetry Ireland Butlers Café Competition, the iYeats, and the Francis Ledwidge awards, and was also shortlisted for the Over The Edge New Writer of the Year; Hennessy Literary Award; Dead Good Poetry; Bradshaw Books; Leaf Books; Poetry Ireland Love Your Bike; and Red Line Book Festival competitions. 'Notice' was first published in the *Stinging Fly* (Housing and Homelessness issue), 'There Was No Funeral' was shortlisted last year but unpublished, apart from in Jessamine's self-published chapbook *Pact.*

Notice

There's no memory in me
of Brighton Square, the half-house flat
my parents shared before the split

then just a shadow, time trapped like a camera flash
of the garage me and mum stayed in
during transit, more a granny-flat she says,
which her school-friend kindly lent us.

A stay in my granny's

before Brabazon Square, the cold corner of a terrace
with too many doors and the ghost
only I saw.

29 Little Mary Street, over an army surplus shop
beside Slattery's, and I can still see the silhouette of a rat
that sat in the bedroom door regularly, and being told to leave
when I was seen on the stairs — this was meant to be 'a student house'
meaning: no kids.

Back to granny's — then out again.
1 Ebeneezer Terrace, a corner house near The Coombe
and in that winter of '82 the snow flowed up to the sky
but I'd started school now, two bus rides away
—the first ever Educate Together—
so we had to move

to a different world,
the salubrious seaside, 71 Albert Road;
we shared the house with one other man, had a back garden
with grass like a forest canopy
but they were selling.

Staying by the sea, 12 Breffni Terrace,
the first in a run of basement flats,
a four-story redbrick beauty of a house
but servants' quarters are gloomy
and the thumping of the landlord's family feet
across our ceiling was a torment
to me, always wanting to be up there
with them, playing, which I often was, until
the day of the smashed plates and tears
and then of course we got the four-weeks' notice
and they got divorced.

Some winter months in my stepdad's family home
while they were away

then a few doors down, another basement,
20A Summerhill Road, where the daughters above
loved knocking on our door
if it was only me there, and running off laughing
or else forcing their way in
to stare and sneer at my crappy room,
and I was terrified of them because —as they made clear—
this was their house.

Further up the same road, 3A,
steep steps down, not a lot of light and when
they were suddenly selling
the auctioneer pushed his way past me into the flat

though I was alone and just thirteen.
Out to the sticks then, 32 Bayview Lawns,
a corner house on a strangely suburban estate, and we had it
for two whole years of my teens,
the walk to and from the Dart to school was a mile
along a harsh stony beach, perfect for smoking and self-absorption,
we chose to leave.

4 Longford Terrace, nice flat with a view of the sea
but the landlord had a daughter
who needed a place more than we did.

Out of home,
27 Lower Drumcondra Road,
under the railway tracks, the bottom floor of a rotten house
that we affectionately called The Pit,
and while we were all dancing one morning
the prefab flat in the back burnt down gloriously
and later the landlord collected his insurance,
that tenant —by good fortune— being put out just beforehand

and around then I fell on my head;
a stay in The Mater followed by appointments,
more appointments and an ambulance chaser,
so though sometimes one eye looked back bigger than the other
the claim was in, and everyone grew impatient
in anticipation of the pay-out,
black mould over the bed, no heating, no hot water,
seven of us paid rent there for another year more.

8 North Frederick Street, a two-room flat at the back
with bars on the windows and a shower in the bedroom,
three of us in it until the landlord spotted my bump
and at eight months pregnant he called round to give me
four-weeks' notice: this place was not suitable
for children, he said kindly, and him and his muscular son
with The Sun in his pocket
stood over me while I scrubbed at the carpet
trying to get the stains out that he said had cost me my deposit,
and I scrubbed with that belly nearly touching the floor

for 400 pounds and still didn't get it.
Carrying black sacks of our lives up the road
after finally finding a flat that would take us
but when I went in for rent allowance they wouldn't allow it,
this place too was unsuitable, they say calmly
but I'm hysterical, all the way back there
to pack up again, almost on the due date
and with no idea where we were going

but someone was moving out from a nice corner house;
27 Primrose Street, and she had a kid too so it would be cool
and for a while it was,
but the mould soon grew on the wall,
gas heating we couldn't afford to use
but the glass coals looked nice with the light on behind them
and we had problems that had nothing to do with walls.
Though before the end of that four-weeks' notice
a skip appeared with the last of our stuff thrown in it
while we were out, the locks changed, and I wept for weeks
over a Moses basket I had wanted to keep.

More fortunate than many, my son and I
were offered back out to the seaside by my mother and husband
and stayed over a year in their two-bedroom flat,
his father soon becoming my ex —
that same night leaving the couch he was surfing
to sleep on the streets, in and around Stephen's Green mostly,
so we'd go in nearly every day on the Dart to see him
and to see him decay.
Pushing the pushchair with dread up the road
craning to get a sight of him first, to wave,
wait till he got up off the cardboard at least
before the pushchair got closer, then one day
we're walking along
nearing another man curled up in a doorway
and my two-year-old boy calls out with joy
There's Daddy!

and coming back to that flat
12 Eden Park, the best yet,

bay windows, no rent-rise or notice
just an incredible lonely view of the sea,
and then my money came through,
the head injury paid off
and we were gone
into the west

and it took years
to learn we can paint the walls, put up shelves, pictures,
or take them down, grow food, shift things around,
that it's allowed — no one is coming to throw us out.

So my children don't know what it's like yet to move, be insecure,
to not know where you're going to be, or for how long,
to keep everything always half unpacked —
but I will never forget.

There Was No Funeral

There was no funeral in the bathroom
when her first unborn slipped into the toilet
unnoticed. So when ten days later, still doubled over,
she was sent for the scan
to confirm she was clean —nothing left
to be infectious— and a nurse snarled the accusation
There's no baby here
as if she was pretending to be pregnant,
there were to be no condolences.

There was no funeral in the bathroom
the second time when she had already
live children to care for,
and though the ambiguous twelve-week-old
foetus was leaving her, desolate,
there wasn't a suggestion of bereavement
counselling, or call for a priest, just painkillers
and an awkward handful of tissues
on the way back out the door.

There was no funeral in the bathroom
the third time when it had been her decision,
just a secret ceremony of her own,
blessing the first specks of it
the day after taking the pills,
and it is possible
to be both grieving and relieved,
knowing that this loss was no worse
than the others
where no one came to sympathise either,
or judge.

Barbara O'Donnell

was born in West Cork in 1975, a publican's daughter, and started working in addition to school at age 13. She worked in several different jobs before training in nursing in 1995. She started in the NHS London, first as a healthcare assistant and porter, and is now working as a sister. Her work has been published in *Atrium Poetry, Ink, Sweat & Tears, Skylight 47, South Bank Poetry* and *Poetry24.*

Airsickness
for Billo

No plastic 1916 Dublin GPO replica
or "Feckin Eejit" fridge magnet.
No Hairy Baby tea towel or
bronze Celtic cross for your wall.

The Reeling in the Years box set might
do it, except they don't carry it anymore.
In any case, you're afraid to see, what
Ireland was like in the year of your birth.

Or the subsequent childhood, where
the black clerical skirt fist ruled and
all that fuss was made, about Gaybo
demonstrating a condom on a banana.

Not long before, women had to bring
the Pill back from the North by train.
No comfort from the good-looking man,
whose wife you might be, if you'd stayed.

The last look at something unreal from
home, to line the pockets of
people who make their living off
preordained, itinerant heartache.

Even the bottle of Dingle Vodka,
sublimation of the national staple, will
only go as far as the blue glass bottom.
Not one of them will do the job.

Lani O'Hanlon

is a dance therapist and author of *Dancing the Rainbow, Holistic Well-Being through Movement* (Mercier Press 2007). She has an MA in creative writing and her work has been published in various literary magazines including *POETRY, Poetry Ireland Review, The Irish Times, Mslexia, Southword* and broadcast on Irish national radio. Her poetry chapbook *The Little Theatre* explores her relationship with her working-class mother, who earned her living as a tap dancer from the 1950s to 1980, and the oppression of women by the Catholic Church and State working together at that time. As a self-employed movement practitioner and writer working in the arts and health, particularly mental health, Lani has written about the current mental health crisis in Ireland and the lack of resources for those who are suffering from oppression, financial hardship, homelessness, domestic and political violence. She is the recipient of numerous bursaries and awards including a Travel and Training bursary from the National Arts Council, to complete a first novel set in Ireland and Greece. 'Until the Young are Reared' was first published in *The Stinging Fly* (Housing and Homelessness Section Issue 37, 2017-2018).

Until the Young are Reared

I

Jackdaws in the chimney, their young
squeaking and mewling into their chests,
parents flying in from the fields, insects
and apple blossoms falling from their beaks.

Swallows skim the crown of my head
as I walk in and out with the laundry,
their clay hive in the corner of the outhouse
above the washing machine.

The birds have taken over the house

Pigeons ate through the wire
we'd placed across the pigeon-hole.
They're in the attic now, gloating,
cooing and coughing.

The other night the chimney caught fire.
You poured water in behind the wooden lintel.

'They've made a bloody bonfire in there.
God knows what they're up to in the attic.'

Paddy Mac came to investigate,
'You can put a cap on one side of the chimney
but maybe we should wait until the young are reared
then we'll seal up the pigeon-hole as well.

I mean you wouldn't like if people came
and sealed up your house and wouldn't let you back in?'
'No,' we agreed, thinking about the split mortgage
'we wouldn't like that. We wouldn't like that at all.'

II

Once upon a time my stilt-walking
circus friend lived in the back of a truck,
reared her young there in the woods,
until the farmer's wife told on them.

The owner of the rented house
said that they had to leave,
my friend was eight and a half months pregnant,
just before Christmas it was.

The seven year old had had a sort of pagan
first holy communion. She wanted a white dress
like everybody else. Celebrating her,
they hung ribbons from the thorn tree.

The owners didn't like that, they didn't like that at all.

'It's impossible for young families,' I said,
'what with the rents and the gombeens.'
'Yes,' she agreed 'they won't let us land
but they won't let us travel either

and pull up at the side of the road or beside the beach.
I mean we're good at that, we can live so simply.'

Bruises Like Countries

Long hair screened Maria's face, turned away
from the camera on his phone —her naked body—
bruises like countries on the ocean of her flesh.
He sent this photograph to a friend,
wrote underneath; 'I have her under control'
and pressed send.

And Maria is with you now as you go about your day
though you wanted to screen your eyes,
like the photograph of that Syrian girl
with her hand covering the eyes of her doll.
You couldn't see that horror, just the child looking
at whatever they were doing but hiding it from her doll.

When they first showed those silent movies
in Ireland, the children and even the adults
went behind the screen to meet the actors
they'd seen. They really thought it was
possible to step through the projection, talk
and shake hands with Charlie Chaplin, Carmencita.

In Greece, in the camp, the children
made an animated film about a bird with a beakful of water
trying to put out a forest fire. 'What are you doing?'
The other birds asked, 'those drops won't help.'
But I'm doing my best' the bird said, so they joined in
and seeing this, the sun began to cry, put out the fire with tears.

You try to reach into the screen, write letters, poems,
share and sign your name over and over, your beakful
of water, and when John comes home from his job
working flat out with the perpetrators
of domestic violence, you make him soup.
Hold him close in the flickering light.

Maeve O'Lynn

was born in the eighties in Belfast. She has lived in Belfast for most of her life and while having had the opportunity to get a PhD and publish her writing, her grandparents left school with no qualifications to work in menial jobs and factories. Her grandparents died in their sixties. Her granny had nine children. Two died shortly after birth; one would be one of Belfast's Bog Meadows Babies. While many things have changed in the last fifty years, in the North we still live with no female bodily autonomy, and this is a link that Maeve's post-human work explores, linking the women of tomorrow with the women of today and with our mothers, grandmothers, and great grandmothers. A key thematic concern in Maeve's work is that women's lives are linked across class and religious divides in the North, and yet "options" are only provided for those who can afford to access them. Canto IV is part of a longer poetry pamphlet for a new exhibition at Sirius Art Centre in Cobh as part of the Xenophon Project, an archive from a post-human future, combining poetic narrative, contemporary arts practice, animation and technology to explore the interstices between art and science. However, it is also a response to the political and social climate we create our work in.

Canto IV

Mapping and exploring
A fairly colourful history
This colonial association,
the harshest penal colony
a handy place to exile political
dissidents, communists, poets, anyone that disagreed
with power:
Fortified, fenced off.
She is still out there somewhere,
We were together the whole time.
I have no theories.
I miss my friend,
Nothing suspicious is found

if she took a pregnancy test in the bathroom
in Heathrow, we have no evidence of this
or what her
feelings on that may have been
I had no reason not to believe, but
I can no longer be certain

what we have here are
a lot of small pieces, fragments really, of information
we may never know
contact was lost
and has not been re-established.
we no longer expect anyone to arrive —
somehow, in this deepest and darkest crevice of the planet,
life,
in all its many forms,
continues with temerity.

Liam O'Neill

was born in Kilkenny, the first of his family to go to college. He worked in engineering for 20 years in London, Spain and Dublin. After becoming redundant in the 2008 financial crash, he retrained as a manufacturing clerk. Disillusioned with working for soulless multinational companies, he now enjoys working with adults with intellectual disabilities in Galway. His work has been published in *The Irish Times, Poetry Ireland Review*, and *Let Us Rise—a commemoration of the Limerick Workers' Soviet, 1919*. He has also written a family history titled *All the days of Winter*, available as an ebook on Amazon UK. 'Railings of Government Buildings' was published previously published in *Let Us Rise; Anthology of the Limerick Soviet 1919*, published in January 2019.

Trickle Down

The rain trickles down my window.
I wait for it to stop, so I can post
a letter and go to the local store
to buy a large tube of instant glue.

Redundant now; my cardboard box of
useless work things sitting tilted in
a makeshift storeroom under the stairs.

I comfort myself with the knowledge
that a job will materialise, though
my demographic may be a disadvantage.

I omit my age from the application form
and alter some stuff as to confuse the
years and make myself seem younger than
the lines on my face testify.

Later, when the rain stops trickling down
the window pane, I post the millionth
application form and then walk to the store
for the glue, with which to fix my shoes.

An engineer gluing his interview shoes
in a so-called 'trickle-down' economy,
the pathos alone would be enough to
make you laugh — until you have to cry.

What are we if not Efficient?

I can put 33 washers on 33 pins
in 60 seconds or less
but there is a robot being shipped
who can do more I guess.
Today, I am told
I'm to be freed from the monotony
of this particular task,
free to retrain for another job
somewhere else —
at my own expense.

The plant manager thanked us
all for our efforts over
the recent, difficult years;
efforts in making the plant
less wasteful, meaning
more efficient, meaning
more profitable, meaning
more profitable for
faceless investors, our
faceless taskmasters,
who always demand more.
And then some.

One of the machine workers
piped up,
(*a man I don't like but usually
has a point*)
The Nazis killed 15,000 Jews
each day in concentration camps
in WW2 — you could say, that
they were efficient too.
The plant manager pretended not to hear
and was escorted
promptly from the podium.

We are to be saved
from the monotony of our jobs,
just like the Jews were saved
from the monotony
of their lives.

Arbeit macht frei —
Work indeed *sets you free*—
but robots and investors
will always set you freer.

The Railings of Government Buildings

We had different shadows in those days;
they cast out long and thin, but that
was under a different Sun, before the
weight of the universe shifted, and we found
ourselves, less humble, less altruistic,
and less significant — than we previously thought.

Our ideologies shifted daily in those days too;
as we marched, walked and chanted. Singing
off key and drinking pots of tea and porter
in backstreet bars and debating over poverty,
equality, and rising up in outrageous protest at the
immoral behaviours of those in authority.

These days, our silhouettes, separated by
distance and time zones, are larger and wider,
as we move slowly and sluggishly along the high
street stores or the housing schemes of suburbia.
Our individualised protests, more silent now,
more subdued, self-injurious and scolding.

Occasionally though, when I find myself in the city,
and passing the railings of government buildings,
a pang rises up inside; a longing to return to the days
of that younger Sun, and to march beside and in-step
with you my trusted friend, and bathe once again,
in the fantastic light of youth, purpose,
          and the demonstrable truth.

Ciarán O' Rourke

has recently finished his studies in Trinity College Dublin, with a thesis focusing on the politics of the American poet, William Carlos Williams. Over the past number of years, he has worked at a number of part-time and casually contracted jobs, including as a shelver, a tutor, a telemarketer, and exams assistant. While in university, he witnessed a drive by college authorities to introduce even more hierarchy and for-profit thinking into university management structures—with the result that he became involved in campaigns for the abolition of student fees, against precarious contracts for postgraduate and non-academic staff, and opposing academic collusion with Israeli weapons companies, among other issues. He has been an active campaigner with People Before Profit, both North and South. His poetry has won numerous prizes and awards, and his first collection, *The Buried Breath*, is available from Irish Pages Press.

Martín Chambi

In memory of Martín Chambi, 1891-1973

In far Peru, where
the fish-metallic rivers steam,

and ten
thousand children

dig the golden earth
in force, for food,

in freedom's name,
a life-wave's crash

away, Martín,
you found your feet

at just fourteen,
and learnt to see.

Impelled by light,
your daughter said,

you set your studio
in reach

of the Incan heights
and peasant skies

you first took breath
beneath, and let them sing.

A dirt-forgotten people
lived within your lens,

and carried on,
with the sun-

beat women
smiling, hauling hay,

the not-quite-quiet
shining

from the Andean giant's
gentle gaze,

the barefoot organist,
his long-boned feet

a slow caress
on pedals made of wood —

his air of luminous
resolve

matched, among
your portraits, only

by the grace of one
red-shawled Miguel,

whose voice, I know,
was heard

in every mud-rich
village of the land,

and whose bones
were later snapped

and slung
in the rising sewerage-streets of Líma,

though you glimpsed his
bright perfection here:

returned
from the famished ridges,

alert to what
the light unfolds,

his tilted face awash,
he grips

between his finger-tops
two trade-forbidden cocoa leaves,

and sits, hunger-firm,
but strong enough

to still, for now,
the baring instruments,

and lift
the sunken heart.

Brunete

In memory of Gerda Taro, 1910-1937

The bursting bullets flung
by two-chinned Franco's smiling men

to pin the heads of children
squatting in the square,

says Langston Hughes, who loved
the rising river-flow

of freedom (jazz) above the rest,
were usually reserved

for the sun-dark beasts of Africa
alone, so fully

did they shake the nerves
and disembowel the flesh:

murder made to mutilate,
the mark of modern times —

a calculation caught and held
in eye-grey revelation

by your blinking fingers, Gerda,
as on the streaming

patchwork floor of the morgue,
or first on the front

in a singeing wind, you stilled
the curling fist and mouth

of innocence itself: a photograph
to document and damn

this rehearsal-round of Hitler's,
Mussolini's morning game...

a death-hung tipping-point
you windowed in Brunete,

witnessing the world of now
(today) and then, until

the smoking fires
fell again — to blot

the gaze of your body,
and rip

the flinchless camera
from your hands.

Karl Parkinson

is a writer from inner-city Dublin. *The Blocks,* his début novel, was published to critical acclaim in 2016 by New Binary Press. In 2013 Wurmpress published his début poetry collection, *Litany of the City and Other Poems,* and his second poetry collection, *Butterflies of a Bad Summer,* was published by Salmon in 2016. His work has appeared in the anthologies, *New Planet Cabaret* (New Island Press) and *If Ever You Go: A Map of Dublin in Poetry and Song* (Dedalus Press), *The Deep Heart's Core: Irish poets revisit a touchstone poem* (Dedalus Press). His work has been published in *The Irish Times* and *RTE Culture, The Dublin Inquirer, The Stinging Fly.*

Poetry Class

In secondary school
there were A classes
and B classes,
I was in a B class,
where they put the dumb kids,
crazy kids,
weirdos,
all from the same
class —
working class.
Justin was
a country boy living in Dublin,
so they put him in with us,
he had more money than us,
he had pockets full of sweets.

We took them from him
by intimidation or force,
'Justin, give us a sweet,'
'Justin, give us your sweets.'

David, he blushed
when he had to read in class,
stuttered,
stumbled,
couldn't pronounce words,
everyone snickered.

Charlie could kick the shit out of everyone
in our class and the other classes,
probably the masters as well,
he got shot dead a few years ago
and left on the Ballymun road.

Nearly everyone had a nickname:
Lamber, Noddy, Parkie, Toweller,
Roger (he had big buck teeth).
Then there was Lovely,
that was his real name,
'That's a lovely jacket, you've got,'
'Lovely goal you scored there,'
'Are you one of the Mr. Men?'

And there were scraps,
thumbtacks on chairs,
chewing gum in your hair,
wedgies on the stairs,
bullies and the bullied,
laughs and howls,
smashed windows,
hundreds of lines to be written,
detention, torture, intimation,
horrible grey uniforms,
chaos, madness,
diesel hash and butane cans in the jacks.
Oh, and some education,
and poetry,
'O stony grey soil of Monaghan
The laugh from my love you thieved.'

I liked it secretly,
I still like it,
and now I'm proclaiming it,
proudly.

I'm a rhythm man,
I'm a rhyme man,
I'm a poet,

a poeta like Mickey Piñero the junkie Christ,
and I'm turning all the chaos in the uniforms,
the torture in the lines,
the windows in the hash,
the howls in the butane gas,
I'm turning all of that
into
poetry.

Did Ya Hear About Mr. Murphy?

Mr. Murphy buys things to fill holes:
Plasma TV
Honda Civic
Playstation 3.
Owns over 100 porno DVDs,
has a variety of imaginary flings:
Blondes with big breasts
Asians who do anal
Black women with the fullest of lips.

Mr. Murphy buys things to fill holes:
smart phones
bags of charlie
compilation CDs
a laptop that can talk
an i-pod that holds ten thousand songs
but there's only five thousand on it.

He's got a Facebook, Twitter and Google +
a dog named Ozzy who pisses under the sofa.
He got let go from the call centre
His girlfriend dumped him for Tommy, the footballer,
he's going places.

His Ma tells him 'Jobs are out there, if ya look'
He burns his thumb with a match and glows with pain.
He puts joints out on his arms
drinks six cans of *Dutch Gold* every night
wanks while watching *Hollyoaks*
wipes the jip with a dirty sock.

He watches *X-Factor*,
Eastenders, reads *The Sun, The Star*,
The Mail, eats waffles, fish fingers
and chicken goujons from the chipper,
smokes *Amber Leaf*,

takes Diazepam to calm his nerves
smokes the gear, every now and again
with the junkie couple from next door.

Mr. Murphy is broken
and no thing will fix him
no drug will fix him.

He is broken
by the sulphur of the match head
by the eyes of ghouls who stare out from windows
by the memory of his father's voice like a whip across his back
by the legs of teenage girls in micro skirts, who stand on the
corner outside the off-licence.

He is broken
on an ocean of smashed glass
on a bed made of barbed wire and razor blades
on a black spoon with wet orchids in his hair and poppies in
his brain.

She was found

cradling a half emptied bottle of vodka,
the opened rim suckling her breast,
alcohol slow
         ly
           drib
              bli
                 ng
                    down.
Blood on her lips,
She was
thirty-six,
She looked
fifty-six.
On the table:
sleeping pills,
a four day old newspaper
and twenty millilitres of phy in a plastic bottle.

Her hair tangled and unwashed,
blood slow
         ly
           drib
              bli
             ng
            down.

Sores, bruises and wounds on her body,
scabs peeling.

She was found
by Trevor Brady
when he kicked in her door on a Friday morning.
She owed me for a quarter ounce of hash,
there was a smell of piss,
her body was cold and stiff,
and I had to take the money out of her pocket,
Trevor said to his mates.

She was found
cradling a half emptied bottle of vodka,
the opened rim suckling her breast,
alcohol slow
       ly
      drib
        bli
          ng
          down.

Ruth Quinlan

grew up in a household where electricity was of the utmost importance. Her father worked as an electrician his entire life and her mother as a clerical officer —both employed by the Irish Electricity Supply Board. With their support, she went on to be the first in the immediate family to receive a third-level education. She was selected for the Poetry Ireland Introductions Series in 2019 and awarded an artist bursary in 2018 by Galway City Council. She won the 2018 Galway University Hospital Arts Trust Poems for Patience competition, the 2018 Blue Nib Summer Chapbook competition, the 2014 Over the Edge New Writer of the Year Award and the 2012 Hennessy Literary Award for First Fiction. Her work has been published by the *Irish Times* and *Irish Independent* amongst others, and nominated for the Forward Poetry Prize.

The Electrician Who Swam Underwater

The electric cable to Valentia Island was laid by my father,
an umbilical coiled from the navel of Portmagee, fed by the furnaces
      of Moneypoint.
He swam the seabed with stolen fire — a rubber-suited, finned
      Prometheus.

Diving, he joined search parties out in dinghies, hunting needles
in a sodden haystack, the honeycomb of Kerry coves.
He hoped/hoped not to find the drowned, the unholy wrecks

pillaged by crabs for bounty of lips, cartilage of noses.
The sea desired their bodies deep amongst the columns of kelp,
laid down on the rubble of cliffs. It gave up its mates reluctantly.

He caught crayfish and lobster, brought them back in netted bags
      submerged in tubs.
When he opened the car we smelled ocean — stowed away to follow
      him home.
The catch soaked in the garage sink but their scrabbling rasped
      through the walls

until our mother lit a camping stove outside to boil the water.
We looked away when she lowered them in, their claws hooking on
      the pot
as she closed the lid. And they screamed, shrieked — until finally,
      they didn't.

One summer, a stingray flicked its tail to pierce his hand with a barb
        that snagged
mid-way — a poisoned crucifixion nail to show the sea would punish
        theft.
The wound closed slowly, a stigma that bled saltwater.

Yet he was happy scarred, content until tempted once, slipping away
to string electric light across the Sakhir desert night. He crawled back
desiccated, laid his palms on the sea's drenched sands, never left again.

Aoife Reilly

is presently setting up her home for self-sufficiency on the edge of the Burren, Co. Galway. In the past, she has worked at a variety of jobs—in factories in Holland, as a farm worker on organic homesteads and market gardens in New Zealand and Australia, and in the area of outdoor education at Brigid's Garden, Galway. She spent a lot of time learning African music and dance and for a while taught that in youth group settings and in schools. She trained both in education and counselling/psychotherapy and am now spends her time on the land, and writing poems.

Unless

you have been seared
by shock,
don't ask me how she died.
Yes, you want to be pleasant, interested even,
but you cannot know this is the wrong question.

Unless you are ready for the answer,
unless you can look at me without flinching
and hold a steady gaze
when I talk to you about suicide,
unless you have been asked to make a statement
to the police one hour after a death,
don't say yes, you're very sorry for my trouble
you know what it's like and all that.

Unless you've had to think
about how people learn to suicide
or had to imagine what goes through
a young doctor's mind
as she asks questions no human
should ever ask another human,
don't tell me you can just imagine how it feels.

Unless you know how it is
to be left in the dark
as it crushes the light,

Just be quiet.

Inferno

"Without hope we live on in desire" Dante, Inferno.

Bless me father for I have sinned.
And long may it stay that way,
being blessed with a love of flesh,
his and mine intertwined,
loving layers of cash, rich cheese and ruby wine,
bless me for the times when I should
have had more longing, more mistakes
and more bloody messing about
in worlds bruised with cherry and chocolate swirls,
which are too few and far between, father.
Bless me for the times I did not allow myself
to be hoisted against the wall enough
by the lover I was not supposed to have
which had incredible seasons of stolen moments,
with crazy kitchen dancing and singing.
Bless me father,
for without hope we live on in desire.

Moya Roddy

grew up in a working-class area of Dublin and left school at 17. The idea of becoming a writer was not on the radar, but after she went to London and did Media Studies at a Poly, she decided to give it a go. What also compelled her was the fact she never came across anyone like herself in the books she read. Her first novel *The Long Way Home* about a young working-class woman who dreams of becoming a dress designer was described in the *Irish Times* as "simply brilliant". Her short story collection *Other People* (Wordsonthestreet) was long-listed for the Frank O'Connor Award. She has been shortlisted for the Hennessy Award and her debut collection *Out of the Ordinary* (Salmon) was shortlisted for the Strong Shine Award. Her work has been broadcast on RTE Radio and Television and on Channel 4. All three of the poems collected here were published in *Out of the Ordinary* (Salmon 2018) and 'The Girls on my Street' was also published in the *Rush Anthology* 2017.

The Girls on my Street

I envied the girls on my street
their slapdash mothers,
cigarettes dangling,
ash falling
while one or other
bent to wipe a child's dirty face,
a lick and promise;
nobody bothered with facecloths
except us culchies.

They didn't mean to be cruel,
the girls on my street,
it was only a bit of fun.
Wasn't I asking for it —
with my red hair, a heart
open as a country road.

Did Your Mother Not Tell You?

Day old chicks for sale!
Day old chicks for sale!
The inside of the man's transit
glows as if summer's arrived,
the sun come down to roost.
As he pockets my pocket-money,
I cup a tiny bird in my hand.

My mother isn't buying —
off-loads the new-born on a scrawny
neighbour who rears fowl.
Through a mesh fence
I spy her ugly brood:
a clutch of rusty hens —
squabbling and pecking,
scratching in dirt —
beady eyes uncaring.
Did your mother not tell you?
she squawks, two days later,
the fox got it.

Watching my mother flip
omelettes, I notice the skin
on her face has begun to sag,
her shins grown scaly. Maybe
growing up isn't all it's cracked
up to be; if the stupid yolk had
lived it would have turned into
one of *them* and who'd remember
it had once been golden
once been part of the sun.

Feeling the Cold

I convinced myself you didn't feel the cold,
out and about in tee shirts in all weathers.
When the rest of us were knee-high in fur boots,
I'd see you push the pram bare-legged in sandals.
You didn't seem to own a decent coat,
bother much with bobble hats or scarves.
It never dawned on me until late one night,
to get a breath of air I pulled the curtains,
in time to see you running from your house,
hair flying, in nothing but a nightie.
You hadn't even time to put on shoes.

Gabriel Rosenstock
was born in postcolonial Ireland. He's a poet, translator, writer for children, essayist, haikuist, tankaist, novelist, playwright and blogger. His latest title is *Glengower: Poems for No One in Irish and English* (The Onslaught Press).

Lucht Oibre
Looking for work sounds almost as bad as finding it.
                                                     Bob Black

Ní gá dhuit ach féachaint ar mo lámha.
Níor dheineas lá oibre ó rugadh mé.
Ní ligfidh mé orm gur dhein.
Níor chuas riamh ag sclábhaíocht i gcistin
Chun bia a réiteach do na boic mhóra

Ná pléascáin a láimhseáil chun tolláin a chruthú
Ná druilire neomatach chun bóithre a dhéanamh
I dtreo is go mbeadh na boic mhóra in ann bogadh thart.

Níor oibríos riamh i dtionscal na harmála
Ag déanamh gunnaí is buamaí
Chun go mbeadh na boic mhóra in ann codladh sámh a fháil
(Agus brabús mór a dhéanamh is iad fá shuan).

Níor oibríos riamh laistiar de bheár
Ná manglaim a chroitheadh do na boic mhóra.

Níor mharcaíos riamh ar chapall folaíochta
Do na boic mhóra, idir úinéirí is traenálaithe.

Ní fhaca adac riamh
Níor cheapas iasc
Níor chrúigh bó
Chun uachtar a dhéanamh do na boic mhóra.

Níor cuireadh riamh i bhfeighil fuaime ná soilse
In amharclann mé chun siamsaíocht nó seachmall
A chur ar fáil do na boic mhóra

Ní file bóna ghoirm ná bóna bháin mé
Agus maidir le bóna bándearg —
Níor thugas aire riamh d'aon bhoc mór
A lámha a mhaisiú
Ná a chuid fadharcán a bhearradh.
Ní rabhas riamh im' rúnaí ar phá íseal.
Dála Julian Assange
Ní fhéadfainn rún a choimeád.

Is file mé.
Níl faic le díol agam.

Pé rud eile é
Ní tráchtearra é an dán seo.
Bíodh sé agat agus fáilte.

Working Class

Looking for work sounds almost as bad as finding it.
                                        Bob Black

All you need to do is look at my hands.
Never did a day's work in my life.
I can't pretend otherwise.
Never slaved in a hot kitchen
Preparing food for my betters

Or handled explosives to create tunnels —
A jackhammer to make roads—
So that my betters can get around.

Haven't worked in an armaments factory
Making guns and bombs
So that my betters can sleep peacefully at night
(Making enormous profits while out for the count).

I've never worked behind a bar
Or shaken cocktails for my betters.

I've never ridden a thoroughbred —
Owned and trained by my betters.

Never seen a hod
Never fished
Never milked a cow
To make cream for my betters.

Never in charge of sound or lighting
In a theatre in order to create a divarshion
Or illusion for my betters.

I'm neither a blue-collar nor white-collar poet
And as for a pink collar —
I never nursed my betters back to health
Manicured their nails
Or shaved their corns.

Never been a low-paid secretary.
Like Julian Assange
I couldn't keep a secret.

I'm a poet.
Nothing to sell.

Whatever else it might be
This poem is not a commodity.
You're welcome to it.

Trevor Sherlock

was born into a working-class family in Galway City and grew up on a council estate. He has performed his poetry at open mic sessions but has not been published yet. Reciting his poetry in public to largely self-declared middle-class audiences reminds him of being a missionary preaching to a largely and sometimes wilfully uninformed flock. Trevor worked in several jobs in both the private and public sector. He also lived and worked in the Netherlands. 'I am a working-class man' is his primary self-definition and his working-class roots and experiences are regular themes in his work. While he is a very broadly educated person in the formal sense, he describes his major portal of learning as coming from travelling—and not really the final destinations, but the journey and the people he met along the way have been his most important educators.

Finders Keepers

Though only a few had actually seen the dog eat the fiver off the road
The whole street came out to watch and wait and wait
Each hoping that they would get there first
When he shat it out
In the next parish, where the great and the good reside
Some would have gutted the dog alive for the exact same prize.

The Great Big Blue Whale in the Room

Sush!
What are you on about?
Paddies aren't like the Brits, you know.
We all drink in the same pubs
And you can go up and talk shite to anyone.
No, the socio-economic circumstances of your birth could never be the
          primary determinant of the course of your life.
Not in this neck of the woods, anyway.
We are all the same in the madhouse together!

Annette Skade

grew up in a council house in Manchester and is proud to be a working-class person. She has lived on the Beara Peninsula in West Cork, Ireland, for many years. Her first collection, *Thimblerig*, was published in 2013, following her receipt of the Cork Review Literary Manuscript prize. She has been published in various magazines in Ireland, the U.K., the U.S. and Australia. She has won and been placed in several international poetry competitions. She is currently doing a PhD on the poetry of Anne Carson at Dublin City University. 'Bringing in the Washing' came third in the Wordsworth Birthday Poetry Competition 2017, and is on the Wordsworth Trust blog.

Threnody

I know why the sea churns.

A woman gets the news,
drops to the chair, floor — further,
the quick in her bleeds out.
She is liquid now, leaching away,
this hour, this day, day-on-day.
At the back of her eyes
a face ebbs and flows:
his lop-sided smile makes room
for her touch,
the tilt of his head
calling drinks at the bar,
wide arms swinging his kit,
their young child,
onto working-man shoulders.

Can God breathe underwater?

Each year a sacrifice:
the man in blue overalls,
flower-blue eyes, who loved his wife
at first sight; the ready-laugh man
collecting glasses in the pub
in off times; the dancer
bending into sound like a squall;
the daredevil larking about

first night back, caught up
in the dizziness of breathing;
the ones who tread water, the ones
who don't know what hit them,
the ones dragged down
in sight of shore. All lost.

They slipped from sight
like water through our hands;
our hands are empty of them,
our mouths are empty of them,
our chests are hollow,
our eyes are expanses
to search.

Fishermen search. Mates, fathers,
brothers, in-laws, cousins,
make late night calculations
where the body might wash up,
rake inlets and coves
along this torn coastline,
fishboxes are body blows,
spars are pins in their eyes.
On stormy days they are too big
for their own kitchens,
too restless for the hearth,
gaze ever on horizon,
for a break in the weather
to renew the search.

What else is there?

Port

The end of a long weekend,
boats tied up, one outside
the other for lack of berths,
make bridges into darkness.

Flat calm. A cut-glass night,
stars catching light. Shadows
of fishermen filter back,
loath to put to sea.

Aboard a boat, unseen,
a man purses his lips,
his low whistle runs
around the harbour's rim.

Others join in,
piping like seabirds
to whistle up a storm,
to keep the men at home.

Bringing In the Washing

Rain whips window
like flex,
we break mid-sentence,
head out.
At the side the washing line
takes off
in wild geese formation,
the prop
tethers and leads
the V.

Hands snatch at
shirt flaps
grown strong against grey sea,
shape shifters
we pin by one cuff:
blue cliff,
chough's wing,
white strand,
creased headland,
tattered island.

We fold them fast into us,
tuck away,
the bundle swells under elbow,
rain-spotted.
And in before they're soaked,
pile all
on the chair while we finish
our tea.
I take my leave of you — as usual,
arms full.

Ross J. Walsh

is a freelance journalist and aspiring poet living in Dublin, Ireland. He has been writing poetry for 10 years. Born in Wexford, he has spent a lot of his time in the North of Donegal or by the sea in Wexford and Waterford, where the landscape and scenery has inspired much of the imagery in his writing. The themes of his work include the history and politics of Ireland, the environment, and personal introspection on human emotion and relationships.

Turf Blocks by the Stove

Earthy, black blocks
by the warming stove.
Its soot-stained glass
affording me a
glimpse into the
fate of what we now
call turf. What once
was life and now gives
comfort to us.

From the sacred
bog we take our fuel,
our ancestors
instead gave to it.
To appease the
Gods they sacrificed
a man whose grave
we burn to heat our
stoves. Are we the

Gods those druids
had in mind? We tame
and strip the bog
whose murky waters
swallowed up their
gifts. We cut and hack
their hallowed land
into these blocks and
then heat our stoves.

Working with Granite

Palms knarled, roughened, with oaken strength
from hours moulding the glittering stone.
Now they rest on a worn pipe that
billows musky low-lying smoke
while the foxy mongrel lies contentedly in the corner.
His workspace is teeming with creations.
A personal Rushmore here and there.
Why stay all day here all alone?
The pipe nearly slips from his smile.
"It passes the time,
and the dog keeps me company".

Black 47 to 17

Ain't no home.
Not on these quiet streets
where the new
gentry lie in wait to
sink their long
vampiric fangs into
your wallet.
Where expensive dwellings
harken back
to Black 47,
when we were
stuffed inside workhouses,
packed tight like
cigarettes in their box,
just waiting
to burn out. The greedy
rub their hands
with glee in much the same
way now as
they did back then. Over
a hundred
and seventy years changed

nothing. The
rich get richer and the
poor grow more
poor, and most of us have
nowhere to
live. For there ain't no home
in Dublin.

Jim Ward

is a native of Salthill, Galway, Ireland. From a solid working-class background, he achieved a scholarship to the local university. He has previously been published in Irish and English for poetry and short stories. His play *Just Guff* won 'Best in the West' at Galway Fringe Festival, 2017 and was performed in Liberty Hall during MayFest 2019. Jim Ward is part of the precariat.

The Second Fall

I read "of man's first disobedience" and what followed
Believing it fixed in time — before time.
That it would not happen again,
The loss of innocence by eating forbidden fruit.
A once-off that tainted all descendants of the banished pair and
          condemned us all to strife.
Till I saw on television the downing of the Berlin Wall
And after, as one by one another Eden fell.

Sold a lie of consumerism; capitalism sanitised, masked as freedom.
They did not understand its workings,
As I still don't the workings of the honeybee.
How a profit is made, the meaning of surplus value,
Their future reminding me of the innocence of lambs ignorant
          of their fate.
Too late to turn back time now even if they could. The monster is
          unleashed
And the question comes to mind…
What serpent was it caused this second fall?

Handy Man
i.m. Joe O'Boyle

Whistling gaily while he worked, melodies not on the Hit Parade
and I am woken early on bright summer mornings
when my aunt would decide the house needed sprucing —
Joe Boyle, his overalls splattered like an artist's palette or as if by Jackson
Pollock, after years of messy toil.
Fearless of heights, he'd call down to me from the tallest summits his
trade brought him, like a steeplejack.
With ladder on shoulders across town he'd cycle to jobs
and race me home from school whenever our bicycles met at dinner time.
A jack-of-all-trades, he could mend windows too — and hang doors
With a handy dexterity everything fell into place, like the perfect magic
          trick.

II

He lost both legs after routine surgery went wrong
(those not as skilled at their trade as he).
His last years spent observing from a wheelchair.
His no longer active body tried to equal his keen mind
till one became prisoner of the other —
and both of life's sour fate.
A half-dozen businesses took on his work, one for each of his skills,
though none could whistle his melodies, or even name them.

Pay Day

As oil fries chips in the kitchen

the smoke envelopes the orange globe hanging from the ceiling

tea-time on Friday —Friday...the goalpost of the week's play— the corner
    shop's milestone.
Already night outside, long winters, the news on the telly.

Raised voices, the sounds loud, then shushed, obeying the score-sheet
    of 'don't let the kids hear'.

UB40 play on my tranny 'I am a one in ten...'

The reek of hops from his breath,
no longer king for a day, the excuses stumble out 'taxes' 'bills' 'I have a
    life too'

'And aren't you in a union?' I hear her ask.

Only words but they hit their target —
the front door slams behind him,

the outside gate creaks on neglected hinges.

Alan Weadick

Since leaving secondary school in the nineteen eighties Weadick has worked in a wide variety of jobs across the construction, retail, health, manufacturing and security sectors, while at the same time being involved as an actor, writer and backstage in the fringe theatre scene of the 1990s. More recently, he has been publishing poetry and short stories in outlets including the *Irish Times, Cyphers, Southword* and *the Honest Ulsterman*. He was a reader at Poetry Ireland's Introductions, has been long and shortlisted for competitions including Listowel Writers week, Strokestown Poetry festival, the National Poetry competition (UK 2017) the Francis McManus short story competition and been nominated for a Hennessy Literary Award (Emerging Poetry, 2016). He continues to work as a security officer in Dublin, where he lives with his wife and two children.

Vespucci Ice Cream (The Line)

On a dream-slick floor I trudge between
the humming, churning vats and *The Line*
where a dozen white linen and plastic-capped women
milk tub after tub of the on-tap gold
streaming from silver faucets
hour after hour, till they run dry after dark.

Days I toss boxes in and out of freezer trucks,
see a brave new world of previously unheard of
seaside towns from a smoke-filled transit cab, collect
a surprising amount of nods, winks and advances
from around posh supermarket *Goods In* entrances.
But it all comes back to the factory floor
with a longing I see mirrored in the drivers' and helpers' faces
as we all drift back there near close of business
to gaze at the women on *The Line*.

Made anything but shapeless in their overalls
they sway a beat or two behind the rhythm of excess,
taming the spiralling swirls of vanilla, rasberry-ripple,
chocolate and banana, gushing in unceasing surfeit;
such grace under the pressure of an unstoppable clock
is something you see every day
but can somehow never get enough of.

Unless it's erased, by the sudden whim of a boss,
a roving manager, or one of the owners, some emperor
of everything, stepping up behind that day's candidate,
one of that line under orders not to waste a drop.
Holding her helpless in his arms,
hands busily out of our sight,
he nuzzles her stiffened neck
or nibbles the lobe of her ear,
with his hips clamped on to hers,
constricting her already tiny orbit —
in that space where you can't hear yourself speak
for the precision-timed grind of noise—
till his moment's hunger is gratified.

And we are sickened, then, us grunts
and fork-lift jockeys of the ice cream business;
queasy with a mouthful of outrage, a splutter of envy
and a few other mystery ingredients
you wouldn't have thought would go together,
but do, every day, like the taste of ice-cream,
the brain-freeze that silently runs whole
glittering universes of work
and a lifetime's work of dreaming
yourself elsewhere, its hands daily upon you.

The Workshop

When the heat miraculously did make waves
and shadowless twos and threes of things
I didn't want to climb or scald on,
the workshop with its underfoot murk
of machines and tools was an eye-rest.
I rarely saw a car deflate itself to a fuming
stop inside those breeze block walls but I did believe
the smoking kitchens of some squat city came
to cool their heels there: More than one
Bain-Marie reclined in grease-stained aprons;
up-ended potato-peelers sang their lowest notes, at a push;
fan-blades lay like a rainforest plane-crash;
cold-steel canopies were lava-blackened.

And my father made his own weather:
inside, through an elephant's graveyard
of scaffolding poles and un-walked planks
the sparks from the orange flame shooting
from gloved fingertips illuminated an underworld
reachable only by way of his black-masked eyes.
He did not need to pick apart what he had on his hands
to master it, completely. As he lay the torch down
and the blue flame sighed at our feet
the storm that had passed over, as they all did,
left us silent and sweat-stung in its wake.
The cauterised scar on the mended machine
mirrored the smiling lips that would emerge
from behind the mask into that idling future
I was careless enough to wish for.

The Quiet Ones

Back in the Old School it must have been thought
that in quiet there resided some powerful magic;

Otherwise how credit our elders' relentless pursuit
of it. Not the ringing silence of the classroom,

counting itself out *fingers on your lips.*
But the quiet that came later with dead wide grins

after the huddle in the factory yard was broken
at the approach of the foreman, for instance,

him or his clueless, blabbermouth nephew;
or the quiet enforced by rattled newspapers,

and dry coughs, by stadium roars and stereo wool-gathering;
the throat-clearing quiet of rooms without books,

or any to speak of; the quiet in refusing not only to speak
but even to read, never mind sing, *ever*, in "public";

a quiet that meant anything but consent
when it couldn't manage exile or master cunning;

a quiet nonetheless accommodating
generation after generation in their showing up

at roll call, absenting themselves from the dawn chorus,
the quiet ones who could tread

the murky water of silent newsreel footage
but who now, having deserted the cemeteries

as definitively as they always have,
are wondering what it is that detains us,

as they gesture unflaggingly from the other side
of our hand-held screens, trying to attract our attention.